Chains of Freedom

Chains of Freedom

Writings of a Redeemed Soul

Heather O'Brien

The resources in this book are provided for informational purposes only and should not be used to replace the specialized training and professional judgment of a health care or mental health care professional. Please always consult a trained professional before making any decision regarding treatment of yourself or others. For more information, contact heatherobrien84@hotmail.com.

ISBN: 9798376441312

Scripture quotations marked (TPT) are from The Passion Translation®. Copyright © 2017, 2018 by Passion & Fire Ministries, Inc. Used by permission. All rights reserved. www.thePassionTranslation.com.

The conversations in the book all come from the author's recollections, though they are not written to represent word-for-word transcripts. Rather, the author has retold them in a way that evokes the feeling and meaning of what was said, and in all instances, the essence of the dialogue is accurate. In order to maintain their anonymity, in some instances, the author has changed the names of individuals and places. The author may also have changed some identifying characteristics and details.

Mom- you taught me how to write and read; fostering a love for words that continues. Thank you for showing me how powerful the written word is while showing me that nothing is more powerful than the Word. I love you.

Karen-my friend and oftentimes the first person read these posts. Thank you for encouraging me to keep writing while gently editing some of the more raw and emotional ones. Love you friendel.

Contents

Acknowledgements | i

Introduction | iii

Psych Ward Scribbles | 1

Ministry School Daze | 21

Jesus, Coffee, and Therapy | 63

The War Writings | 113

Acknowledgements

Always God first. These wouldn't exist without Him. I would simply be still scribbling in a psych ward somewhere. You gave me an ability to create with words and I won't forget it's Your ability not mine.

My parents who so graciously let me sit around in my jammies at the kitchen table or in the basement, typing and mumbling, day after day. Plus editing and assuaging my fears that I don't know what I'm doing half the time (ok, most of the time).

Albus. Yeah I'm going to thank my dog! He helps make sure I get out of my pj's and do some exercise each day.

Rachel Newhouse, formatting really should be a four letter word but you graciously keep showing me how to do things and doing the parts that kerfuffle me. Which really is most of it. Thanks all the encouragement, food, and yes, that dang formatting.

Introduction

If you would have told me nine years ago that I would become a writer, I probably would have laughed and then smacked you. Because that's the type of things that people who are labelled unstable do. I was completely broken mentally. I heard voices and saw things that weren't real. I stared at walls and got lost in stores. Medications were changed almost constantly trying to get the cocktail right. There was no way that I was able to write, I was barely verbally coherent on good days.

Then five years ago, I had a deep encounter with the Living God. Everything about my life changed seemingly almost overnight. The voices began to recede, the imaginary "friends" (let's call them for what they are, evil spirits) were silenced. I began to learn who I am; that my identity is rooted in God. These writings are the ups and downs of the some of the journey. Enjoy.

Psych Ward Scribbles

The following are the very first of my writings done after I began to follow Jesus. They were usually written late at night while I worked the late shift at a children's psychiatric ward. It was an interesting place to begin a writing path, but I could feel God's Presence so strongly in there. He is close to the broken, especially when we don't understand how.

Surrounded

I'm surrounded by things that shouldn't be. Tiny bodies who twitch not because of pleasant dreams but because at night memories of their past reality replay over and over. Beautiful eyes whose orbs reflect only fear, confusion, and madness. They have lived a thousand years in less than a decade.

I'm surrounded by things that shouldn't be. Teenage bodies who twitch not from excitement but withdrawals. Beautiful eyes whose orbs dilate and contract with their craving, reflecting addiction, mental illness, and a world-weary gaze. They aren't yet twenty but many count them as dead already.

I'm surrounded by things that shouldn't be. Adult bodies who twitch because of a constant state of hyper awareness. Beautiful eyes whose orbs reflect only PTSD, compassion-fatigue, and an ever-widening gap disconnecting them from their family. They are different ages and yet they are all old.

I'm surrounded by all these things that should be, yet I'm bringing into this building exactly what will be! My body doesn't twitch with anxiety but with excitement and joy. My eyes don't reflect my own; instead, they show that I am simply a place where Jesus has made a home. My age doesn't matter as the ageless Holy Spirit sings His healing song through me, ordering, "Light Be!"

Buckets

Buckets of soil passing from Your Hands to mine.

To till or to cover this little seed of mine.

Options, options-what to do with this soil handed down from You?

Smother fires, that's what I could do.

Cover flames to rescue others

Or perhaps create steps to help me walk out of my grave.

But this can't be for only me in my cave.

Maybe it's supposed to do a bit of everything.

Cover my seed, smother flames, make steps, the whole thing.

After all, who said I only get one bucket?

Ghosts

I saw a ghost today. It was brief, but I saw a flash of her in my reflection. Anger shining brilliant on her face; stone set and ready to fight. I blinked and she was gone; was it the light or was she still in there somewhere?

I saw a ghost today. It was momentary, but there she was in a windowpane. Bent in depression, head filled with whispering lies. Visible one second and gone the next; but still I wonder, is she wandering around ready to come out again?

I saw a ghost today. Not in my reflection, but in another face. That flash of fury, resolve set; I know that look, I remember it well. I won't rage back; instead let me show you where to find Peace. Can you swallow your anger enough to try?

I saw a ghost today. She almost slipped by in the crowd, her slouching walk and exhausted steps hiding her from others. I didn't miss you; I can still see you clearly. Come meet the One who can heal your mental agony. Will you push back your fear enough to try?

I see ghosts every day. I see them in the cashier, the soccer mom in a van, the tattooed veteran, the guy on the street corner, the TV, the news; they are everywhere. They are haunting, reminders of the life I once knew and hated. Physical specters each carrying their own regrets, shames, pasts, and pains. What more can I do? Or am I too afraid to find out?

You see ghosts every day. Not of who You ever were, but of the creation You designed. Bubbling rage, broken gait, tortured gaze; You never made us to live this way. Even after our failings and mistakes, You created a path to Your peace and healing. Why are we so afraid to set aside our division and contempt for each other? Why does Your healing terrify the most broken?

We all see ghosts every day. They surround us, but we don't have to let them stay this way. Douse anger with the love of Jesus. Be the hand the Great Physician can use to fix the crushed, rejected people society overlooks. Is this something we are willing to do? Or have we decided to settle for what God never intended us to become, crippled and dead to each other?

Dead Alive!

I'm alive today; five years ago I didn't want to be. I thought the best of my life was already past. Thirty years old but I felt a hundred. My life was in shambles, my sin was no longer "fun."

I'm alive today; five years ago I didn't want to be. No, my heart didn't stop or my breathing cease, but I was solidly dead inside. Doctors gave me medicines and therapy, but life was just a flicker at best.

I'm alive today; five years ago I didn't want to be. Waking in the hospital was yet another stabbing reminder of my failures. I was so pitiful I couldn't even die right. So I contented myself to just exist.

I'm alive today; five years ago I didn't want to be. I existed, but only recently did I find Life. Jesus, Creator of life, breathing fire back into me. Restoring, restructuring, and redeeming the shambles that was Heather.

I'm alive today! Five years ago I didn't want to be, but it wasn't until I asked for Life did I really die. No, my heart didn't stop, instead it is being shaped back into tender again. My breathing never ended, but I now inhale the very Spirit of God daily.

I'm alive today! Five years ago is done and over; that shameful sting is dead. Now I die daily to me and live solely for God. I'm standing, breathing, living proof that Jesus can rescue anyone, especially those bent on death. Today, I look death in the face, grin, and say: I'm alive today!!

The Fog

I'm losing it, the fog swirls through my brain, nothing makes sense and darkness sets in. I was told this would happen. Doctors who mean well when they told me that when my brain snapped again just check in to the hospital. Never if, never a possible positive, always when and a phone number to call.

This time it seems like it won't end. It's worse/better than last time. I'm not in a hospital but I'm also not able to be left alone. Overwhelming terror, fog and voices that I know aren't real, but they are so loud it's hard to remember that, much less any conversation I'm trying to have.

One "good" day equals at least two bad ones. How long will this last? God, why aren't you with me, and why aren't You making it stop? Is this pay back for all the years I forsook You and did what I wanted? No! I shake my head! That isn't my brain thinking, it's another voice and it's a lie. But wait, if that's a lie then some of these other thoughts must be too.

What other lies am I being told and how can I tell what's true? A small light begins to pierce the haze. A voice, "I'm here, I never left you; even in the dark I'm right there with you." The foggy voices cease to speak when His voice does. For a moment everything clears. I see Him; Jesus is walking right with me, arms around me making sure I don't fall or slip. I know the fog isn't completely gone, but it's not as strong as before, I'm learning to discern the lies from truth.

The real truth is He has been here the whole time. At no time was/am I alone. That voice telling me no one hears me must be a lie too! Still there are many others waiting to squawk their poison. "Insane, you're insane, yes there are lies in your head because your head is broken and can never be trusted. Insanity is your present and future!"

Too much, it's all too much. I can't shake it out of my head and I can't make it stop yelling. "But I can," I hear You whisper. You still haven't left, You're still right beside me. "I can make it stop, you gave your life to Me; you turned your body, soul, and mind over to Me at salvation. Your mind is no longer yours to lose because I am in possession of it. Will you trust Me enough to put all your broken pieces back together?"

You've taken my past, dear God what did you do?
You've taken it, traded it for something new.
The pieces, memories are all still there,
But now there is no poison, no jagged edges to rip my soul bare.
I can clearly see every thought and sin,
But no longer do I cringe within.
Instead, I rejoice for over every sin I see redemption.
I see You stretching out Your mighty hand to bring me salvation.
In desperation I grabbed ahold of You.
Now in joyous declaration I vow to never let go of You!
Take me, mold me, use me!
Let my past be proof of your love song!

Handprints

Handprints are all over me. Some big taking up large spaces while others are so small, they don't even look like a hand. Others are barely visible, just light touches that are imprinted, yet some are stained dark and look like a blemish that never fades.

Handprints are all over me. I see my mother and father's prints, they are always encircling my heart. Their prints aren't dark, but they are deep, down the very depths of me. With every encouraging word, every hug, kiss, and chat, their prints sink a little deeper into the core of me.

Handprints are all over me. I see my first friend's tiny prints, worn and faded by the years of distance. But they are still there, covering tiny little marks made by bullies. Her prints were the first to show me that good prints can cover bad ones.

Handprints are all over me. I see two big ones that are finally beginning to heal. They aren't even shaped like hands but like two tall towers; these are the prints of an unseen enemy. Until this day I never realized that strangers could leave handprints, especially ones so deep. These are also the first prints that I purposely kept reopening over and over, never allowing them to heal.

Handprints are all over me. The more I look, the more I see. The fading one, left by a command team abandoning their people in war to go home first. The sharper fresh one from a youth who had such hope for her life and we helped her turn it around only to have it violently ripped away by the drug she fought so hard against. The good ones, the bad ones, there are so many that at times I feel like they are choking me.

Handprints are all over me! I can't wipe, scrub, or wash them away. They are a part of me and until recently I thought it had to stay this way. But now I see Your Handprints, covering, removing, and healing these dark blemishes. Your Handprints, nail-scarred and gentle, creating new flesh where my wounds were, bringing life back to the dead areas, allowing me to feel again. Now I rejoice because Your Handprints are all over me!

Little black sheep,
you're not that different from the rest of the herd.

Head, feet, body the same as the white ones. The "normal" ones.

So, you don't match the rest of the herd,
I know, I made you different.

Little black sheep, surrounded by many but you still feel alone.

A simple color divides you only in your mind.
I see your "difference" as beauty.

Don't you know I'm the Creator of all colors?

Little black sheep,
your difference is the very reason I picked this plan for you.

You can go where the rest of the flock can't.

Where they're uncomfortable is where
I've created you to feel at home.
Little black sheep, you're not that different from the rest.

Hurting, shunned, and unwelcome-
the world is full of little black sheep.

You, my little lamb,
understand and aren't afraid to reach out to them.

And this is why I made you, my little black sheep.

Broken: Reduced to fragments, ruptured, torn, not functioning properly.

These are but a few of the definitions for this word. This word that has been applied to my brain and emotions by doctors, therapists, friends, even myself.

Broken; not functioning properly. An accurate description of my life before God.

Most of the world sees me and they see broken. A mind that wanders from time to time, that can't handle loud noises or sudden movements. To them, broken is correct in describing how just being around people is hard sometimes or why I sometimes shut down in public places. I might be having a spacy or foggy moment, but I see it – the couple who looks at me oddly, the woman who mumbles about walking behind "slow people." It would bother me if I were able to just remember what bothered looked and sounded like. So yes, I understand that according to this definition I am broken.

But it's correct in definition for after I surrendered my life, too. I no longer function properly like much of the rest of the world.

Broken: changing direction abruptly, trained, reduced to submission.

Salvation is an inherent act of submission; your life is suddenly changed from that point on, everything is different. I have now given up my rights; in one single act I've changed the outcome of my life. I am broken; submitted to the one living King. I've stepped aside to allow Him full control of my life, wherever He goes so go I; I am broken. But unlike what so many others have told me, I am not broken as in crippled or incapacitated. Rather I am broken like a soldier in boot camp or pre-deployment training who is honed into battle readiness; old traits, mindsets, and habits have been broken away to make me into something better, a soldier ready for war. This brokenness is what makes me a warrior. So yes, I'm broken on more than just one level, but I choose to see it from only God's view.

Healed by Wounds

For years I hated You. I despised Your name, refused to even say Your name unless it was a curse. My sword held high, I attacked You and anyone who defended You. Family or friend, neither mattered if they stood up for You. I cut relationships, slashed familial bonds just to attack You. In my childish anger, I never noticed Your response to my strikes; every time, each instance You had Your hand reached out to reconcile.

Bah! What pitiful and weak god would try to reconnect with someone who vowed to hate Him?! My brain couldn't comprehend the depth of that type of strength, so I attacked again. Swings and jabs, I called You bigoted, useless, and ancient; my rancor knew no limits and I now expanded my contempt to whole churches and congregations. Weak-willed and minded people, is what I would yell and sneer, thrusting my sword at their hearts. Still You showed no wounds, no evidence of my stabs and thrusts.

Frustrated, I turned to the most extreme thing I could do. "You call Yourself the Creator of life?! Well, watch me die," I bellowed to the heavens. Alas, this failed too! My final attempt to kill You had made me severely wound myself. Crippled and in anguish, my screams of rage slowed until only a quiet whimper remained. Suddenly I saw Your hand reaching to me, on the forearm a long ugly scar. That couldn't be from me, it was much too old; despite all those years of attacking You, suddenly I didn't want You to be hurt. With a shock, I realized I didn't want to be the one who hurt You either.

As I slowly began to reach out my hand to Yours, my wound gave a nasty sharp spasm. Looking down I gasped; stabs, jabs, and thrusts from a sword were all over me. How could this be? Every cut, every swing I aimed at You had injured me. My actions of hate aimed at You were killing me! In despair, I lunged and grasped Your hand, even though I just knew You would likely fling me away. A drop of blood hit me and then another, falling neatly into my wounds. I looked for its source; with a jolt I realized Your scar had opened, Your blood falling into my lacerations. What is this?! Where each drop fell, the cuts began to heal; the trauma I inflicted on myself being repaired by Yours.

You weren't weak at all! Oh, the strength and control You must have, waiting for just this moment! You're the God who is truly slow to anger and quick to reconciliation. It's not weakness to wait for Your wayward, tantrum-throwing children to reach for You. How awful it must have been for You to not reach down and forcibly stop me from the harm I was inflicting on myself. Yet You did. With fortitude and love, You waited until I was ready; until I had finally had enough of me and was ready for You. Instead of hating me back, You showed Your love by opening Your own scars to heal me. Expecting Your rejection, I found only true acceptance when I grabbed Your hand and You pulled me into Your arms.

Dips and swirls. Some days my brain works fine; other days it's like a broken recorder stuck on a song, scratchy and repeating. Images flash faster and faster, blurring until I can't separate past from present, memory from confused reality. I don't ask why anymore because why is irrelevant. Genetics, trauma, or self-induced bad living, it doesn't really matter, dips and swirls are what my brain now does.

Talk and jabber. So many times people's voices blend into a painful cacophony of bird cries, "Instant healing!" They squawk, "it happens, accept it, believe harder!" They mean well but don't they understand I'm believing as hard as I can? Medical personnel chirp statistics of hospitalizations, suicide, and med changes as if failure is my only future. Very few realize that sometimes it's ok to fly a little or crash a little. At least in the aftermath the talk and jabber in my head is momentarily quiet.

Dips and swirls, talk and jabber-in between the roller coaster ride and continual noise there is You. Certain, warm, and gentle, Your Presence begins to still the storm. You promise that even in the dips and swirls, You are with me. Your quiet soothing Voice commands peace to the constant talk and jabber in my mind.

Slowly everything stills; I am at rest.

Dips and swirls, talk and jabber, no matter how many times they rise, You have promised to be my center point, my constant, who will never leave me.

Chains of Freedom

Once I wanted to be free. I set out to find freedom anywhere I could. "I could be free out partying," I thought. Having a good time, making new friends, drinking, what could go wrong? Clink, Clank! My search yielded only a chain bound tightly to my jaw and brain. Addiction had just made a new slave.

Next, I turned to the "noble" art: combat. What could be more freeing than saving or taking life? What a rush it would be, after that I would truly be free! Clink, Clank! The chains of violence, anger, and hatred rattled as they settled around my soul. My freedom search was beginning to slow me down.

Love, that was what I was missing! So away I hobbled looking for a companion to complete my missing pieces. The ability to pick my own partner, the ultimate freedom of choice! Clink, Clank! Homosexuality loudly snapped shut around my heart. Freedom slowed me to a crawl.

These chains were painful and crippling my walk! Aha, therapy would solve my problems! A few talks, a couple pills, then these chains would leave. Clink, Clank! PTSD, Bipolar, BPD, Adjustment Disorder; labels flying at me and chains landing in my brain. Madness began to whisper terrifying lies of insanity to my mind, heart, and soul.

Desperate now, I wandered aimlessly, there was only one more step I could think of to make me free. Death, the ultimate freedom! In death, no one could rule me then. Snap! Suicide's chains rattled through the other chains' loops and then tied me to the floor. In agony, I lay unable to move. Addiction, Hatred, Violence, Homosexuality, Madness, and Suicide barely let me breathe. My search for freedom had left me in soul crushing chains!

As I lay, gasping and waiting for death, I heard a still small voice; one I thought I would never hear again. "I'm still here, waiting for you." "But God," I cried, "It can't be true, you can't still love me, I'm broken, filthy, and unable to break free." "Trust Me, Call on Me, and then just watch and see." One deep, ragged breath and I screamed, "Jesus come save me!" Clank, Snap, Pop! The chains all began to drop, as God breathed new life into me. In my Father's embrace I am truly set free.

Ministry School Daze

I began to write even more while I was in my church's School of Ministry. Theology and clarity began to flow as I learned more about God. Even as I understood more, I realized how loving our God is and that theology gets a bad reputation as showing a punitive God. But what it shows is a powerful God and that scares people. I wanted to put into words the love and might I felt from Him; two seeming opposites that prove the truth of each other.

Armor Exchange

I've worn many types of battle rattle in my life but this suit is different. No Kevlar, SAPI plates, bulky blast vests, or chin straps that chafe anymore; this outfit is made perfectly fitted and suited for only me. Many people will scoff when I say God is the craftsman, but I'm quickly recognizing He makes only the best for His children.

In place of a web belt holding a radio, drop holster, and gas mask is a belt with one simple item: truth. The truth of who I am; a daughter of the King, an overcomer, a powerful truth speaker. More importantly the truth of who God is; unconquerable King, I AM THAT I AM, fierce protector and defender of His children. This truth-belt strengthens my spine into straight attention. With it on, I am never bent and certainly not broken.

In place of a Molle vest laden with ammo magazines, binoculars, and Gerber knives is a singular breastplate etched with the word holiness. This plate covers my upper body with special attention over the heart. Holiness, this word conveys the very depth of God's character and He has placed it on me! He has declared that regardless of my past, He has found me holy because of Jesus' sacrifice. Blood payment was made for my sins and I can live with my King in holiness.

In place of my riot shield, cracked, chipped, and gross from hate-filled fights, I have been gifted a new shield of faith. Faith wraps around me and doesn't allow a single arrow in. My faith is in my God who sees me, comes to my aid, and never lets me be put to shame. My growing faith is that I am truly His daughter and walk with His power and authority. Never again will my enemy's arrows pierce this shield.

In place of my Kevlar helmet, the one that is split from rocks and metal pipes, I now wear a salvation helmet. It's no one-time salvation, not this helmet, it's God's ever present salvation. It's healing, restoration, redemption, and deliverance all wrapped into one. And it's constantly doing all these things, not just stopping arrows but renewing my mind and body as well. God's salvation helmet cannot be cracked or broken; I am in perfect safety.

In place of my old combat boots, stained with dirt, blood, and a hundred other horrors, I now have boots of peace. Not the peace that I was taught in the old days; the one that meant weakness, bribery, and compromise, the peace that I once sneered at. No this peace is shalom, it's complete wholeness, soundness, nothing missing, nothing broken. These boots walk forward and gain ground bringing peace to all around. These peace boots bring victory.

In place of my M-4, decked out with infrared, scopes, and even more magazine holders, I now receive a sword. M-4s, pistols, grenade launchers, machine guns, I've carried them all, but nothing compares to this priceless treasure. My sword, the spoken word of God, cuts through not flesh but spirit. No longer do I leave death and pain in my wake; instead I speak God's life-giving breath over people. I give joy where I once only gave despair, blessing instead of a curse. My foes are different too, no longer do I look at a people group and see enemies or a country and wish it death. Now I see the spirit behind the actions and it's them that I swing my Bible sword at. God's Word has never known defeat and it's not going to happen now!

I've worn many types of battle rattle in my life, but this suit of armor is incredibly different. I joyfully drop my armor of old, the stuff that broke, snapped, faded, and let injuries occur. It was all I had for so long but it isn't adequate for the long-term. I accepted a new outfit that cannot fall apart or be penetrated and it heals while it protects. The awesome thing is my suit is not one-of-a-kind; God has one made for you, too. Will you put it on?

The Best Time

"This is the best time of your life!" Friends and teachers chant this over and over in some weird high school mantra. This is my best time? At 18 and newly graduated I'm supposed to believe my life is now only downhill. There has to be more to life than this.

"This is the best time of your life!" My sergeant bellows this with sadistic glee. Forget high school, this is my best time; body splayed and crawling in the mud, pretending that I'm not almost licking the boot laying in front of my face. I still hold out hope that there is more than this.

"This is the best time of my life!" I crow as I relish the daily violence that comes from living in a war zone. Riots, death, savage acts that only further dehumanize me and humanity; this is my daily bread. Nothing could outrush the volatile excitement of this. What could ever be more than this?

"That was the best time of your life." The words endlessly circle through my head as I listlessly hear yet another doctor talk about another medicine. I was right, back then was my best time, nothing else will compare. Now I can only exist from year to year until I escape earth. Is this really all that I can hope for?

"This is the best time of your life!" God's voice thunders from the heavens, in that instant my eyes were opened! This is what I was made for, serving Him. Every day now makes my best time eternity long. This is what I've been looking for all along. It can't be filled in graduations, boot camps, deployments, or pills; instead it's filled in serving my Savior-King every day. This is more than I could ever dream or hope for! Are you willing to give Him a try?

Are We Ready Yet?

Have you awakened yet? You were once called the sleeping giant, but Church, while you slept you grew weak and small. Young people left you by the droves and you simply snuggled deeper in your dreams. Now people are beating on your walls, begging for help, dying from lack of love. Unplug your ears! Lift your head, awaken oh sleeper, arise before you succumb to death!

Are you desperate yet? You called yourself history makers, swore to always seek Me. What happened? Did it get too easy to just go with the flow instead of pave the way? Look where the flow has led you, violence, anger, hatred. But I can still see it in you, that ember, a small flame; stoke it with desperation, fan it with a determination to seek Me. Seek and you will find; I will pour Myself out again if you would only reach for me. I want to be found!

Have you linked arms with each other yet? You disconnected from Me; is it any wonder that you can't seem to agree with each other? Pro-gun, no-gun, Antifa, BLM (Black and Blue), kneel, stand, Republican, Democrat, the lists of division send you to early graves. Belong to My group once again; here every life has value, even those you don't agree with. Stop looking at your differences! I am the Creator of all life, I make you all different to show different facets of My own creativity!

How bad do you want revival?! Not a big church gathering or wild service, but the deep revival you so badly need. One that knows no denomination, no particular church, but sweeps through every part of your being! Are you willing to say, "Start with me!" If not now, then when? How many more sad days and wails of grief must you endure before you say, "Enough! I refuse to hate anymore, even those who would deserve it. I will love like Jesus until Heaven invades earth!"

Psalms 144:5- "Step down from heaven, Lord,
and come down!"

Who are you?

Who are you? A sinner now saved; lost lamb carried home by the Great Shepherd. Such beautiful words and lovely images but is that where it stops? A prayer, church attendance, and maybe some community potlucks; is there nothing more to become? You gave Him your heart but maybe there is more to be had. You have options now! You can be whoever God wants you to be, nothing is out of reach. Find your identity in Christ; don't do but just be, this is where it gets tricky.

Who are you? Maybe you're little orphan Annie. You said the prayer and believed it too but somehow you can't get past the point that God loves you. Your soul feels parentless, wandering, and lost even as God calls you His. You try to do things to please God and others but you never feel truly accepted. Even when you know better you still believe God will leave you someday. "Woe is me" is your underlying attitude and heart's cry. Remember orphan Annie, what you feel isn't always accurate or true. You have a Father whether you "feel" Him or not. Feelings never outweigh facts.

Who are you? Well hello Oliver Twist! You're not exactly an orphan, you realize you have a familial figure in God. Not a parent exactly but someone who will look out for you if you grovel well. Your days are spent looking for ways to satisfy God's supposedly intensely strict standards. You will beg, borrow, and steal whatever you can to get what you think everyone else has. You think everyone else dislikes you because secretly you dislike most of them. "Please sir, can I have some more" is the bread and butter of your existence. Don't be confused, Oliver, God wants us to rely on Him but not just stick our hands out, greedy for more, more, more.

Who are you? Head up, shoulders set, you strut into the room a perfect image of how a Christian should be, at least on the outside. You are the Rosie the Riveter of Christianity! You can perform, strive, and labor with the best of them. Nothing is too hard for you to do, too small for you to notice, or too big for you to accomplish; "I can do it" is your working motto! But deep inside you know it's a sham. You're exhausted, overwhelmed, and overstressed, but this is Christianity right? Strive, strive, strive to pay off your eternal debt of salvation. When you hear about God's rest you secretly believe that's a lie; God doesn't want rest only work, well at least for you. Laboring Rosie, remember that God's yoke is easy and His burden is light. Not because you're strong enough to do everything but because He does it with you.

Who are you? Orphans, beggars, and laborers so often we think these are the only categories but there is one more, one we secretly long to be and yet it terrifies us. It's quite simple and overwhelmingly profound at one time. A child, a son or daughter of God Almighty. I can see you agreeing and rolling your eyes at the same time, but don't get religious now, think about those words. God's child, having His Holy Spirit in you, not even King David or Moses got that.

Who are you? You are His adopted children with the full rights and responsibilities as a member of His family. Set aside your orphan mentality, begging, and laboring ways. You are now a member of Abraham's family and under the same blessing God gave him! You are meant for more than just wallowing in past mistakes and sins; let go of what you despise and just be His child! You became His child at salvation whether you fully believe it or not; God does and He loves you as His own. Let that become who you are; His heir fully and completely. It's more than enough and all we are ever called to be.

Simply His.

Becoming Alive

When I saw you coming towards me, I was terrified. God of gods striding my way, mighty and powerful, nothing could stop You. Were You angry? Did You come to punish me for all my wrongs? In fear, I shrank away from You. I knew You were the God who couldn't stand sin. The One who destroyed cities, armies, and civilizations whenever You got annoyed with them. At least that's what I'd been told. So as You came close, I backed away. Your promise of freedom seemed like death to me.

Standing before me, You stooped down and gently tried to take my hands. Each time You reached Your hands out, I slapped them away. I might be completely chained and unable to run but I refused to surrender. I had listened to one smooth talker once before and look where it got me. Isolated, chained, tortured by my past, present, and hoping to have no future. No! I won't let myself get taken again! I never noticed that the more I pulled away from You, the tighter the chains got.

Still, You didn't leave even as I lay gasping for air. You reached for me again and I knew this was the last time; not because You would quit but because I couldn't live like this anymore. The choice slipped into sharp focus: die in chains, defeated, and ruined or reach for You and see what might happen. Sure I might die but I was already at death's door. In his haste to destroy and kill, the enemy had recklessly pushed me right back to You. Timidly, I touched Your outstretched hand when it drew close. It was warm and surprisingly tender, not how I had envisioned the King of hosts, angry God of the harsh religious system, would be. Instead

I was utterly enveloped by the King of hosts, almighty God, infinite in power yet caring enough to remember me.

The chains began to loosen then fall as You poured life into me. Full life, abundant life! The type of life that cuts through death with laughter and praise! Life so overflowing that it pours out of my every movement and word; I cannot help but spread it everywhere. You have even made me a daughter with all the rights, privileges, and responsibilities of Your royalty. I am now free, fully alive, and adopted! And to think all this time I thought You wanted to harm me! I was so chained, that I viewed Your freedom as evil; a spine-chilling unknown that was death instead of the handcuffs suffocating my soul.

As a new daughter of Jehovah, I have an announcement. The King of angel armies is not angry at us! His enemies are the very demons and devils that tie us down and kill. The horrifying destruction He unleashes are on them not us! In fact the shame and embarrassment those oppressors use to shackle us are nothing more than they're own regrets. We are guilty but the High King-Judge is willing to set aside the verdict; Jesus has already paid our guilt judgement. In this Kingdom, the guilty go free! The question then is will you reach out for Him and life or will you view His outstretched hands as punitive and abusive?

Revival Rain

Send Your revival rain! We sing it, we shout it, but what does it look like? Is it a gentle summer drizzle that moistens the ground but doesn't really seep in? I don't think so for when revival hits nothing and no one is ever the same. People are forever changed for better or for worse; they cannot stay the same. It's about how deep we let You saturate us. We can choose to stop short, to never reach the full rain.

Send Your revival rain! Maybe it's more like a week long rain that fills all the flower beds and flows deep into tree roots. Sounds pleasant, some good outpourings, healings, church attendance grows. This must be it, the wild reign of Your Presence in our nice, safe, religionized churches. People are changing, well at least during church time, but that's what matters right? This must be the revival You are sending us because it's the only one we are praying for, predictable and routine.

Send Your revival rain! I see the cloud in the distance, growing by the second. When it hits it won't be a simple cloudburst or even a weeklong shower, this is a hurricane with torrential flooding! This water won't gently fill a flower pot or softly soak into the ground; this is flood water that fills roads and topples buildings! This can't be Your revival rain, it's strong, overwhelming, uncontainable, and even destructive. God, you would never want to send a revival that would destroy our religiosity and denominations, right? Without all our petty divisions, how would we ever find out which of us You like best?

Send Your revival rain! Jehovah, sweep through our churches! Awaken us to You once again, awaken us to Your call once again. We are tired of the stagnant deterioration floating in our services, flood us, destroy long-held wrong beliefs that separate us from each other and You! Rain down, flood the foundations and crack, pull, rip it down until our foundation is You alone! Overwhelm us until all we see is You. I can hear it in the distance, the pitter-patter of raindrops. Revival is coming. Will you welcome it or shun it? Either way you cannot stay unchanged.

God of Mountains

Who told you this was a mountain? I crafted the earth, each hill, crack, and crevice; I decide what stands tall and what topples. I make the mountain ranges, in all their majestic glory, towering over swathes of land, visible for hundreds of miles. Yet I also care enough to make the fairyfly almost smaller than the eye can see; each wing, leg, and entire internal system less than a single millimeter in entirety. I am the God of both towering rock and tiny creatures; I decide what makes a mountain.

Who told you this was a mountain? Mountains are granite rock, solid and unmoving unless I decide otherwise. I am Lord of the lovely autumn air with its crisp, sharp air shimmering with promise of a lovely day. And I am Lord of the torrential downpour that turns mountains to rivers of mud, dislodging the very foundation of the peaks and sliding them into the seas. With a whisk of my hand, winds rip through the bluffs, decimating its face. I am the God of the gentle days and rough weather; I decide what makes a mountain.

Who told you this was a mountain? Some mountains have been hollowed out in the middle. Years of hot lava running through them has created grooves through the center. With a single eruption this mountain blows itself up. Some molehills act like mountains too, refusing to leave, defiantly growing in your yard until a quick stomp shatters the mountainous illusion. In the end it was no better than the volcano, big and bad, but utterly hollow. I am the God of the death spewing volcano and the frivolous little molehill; I decide what makes a mountain.

Who told you this was a mountain? Anxiety, financial crisis, panic, divorce, rage, sickness, these are just rocks. Granite yes, and when they are stacked up they loom high in your eyes. But I don't look from your point of view. In my eyes these are just molehills, little and hollow. You see Everest, I see a pebble. Use my faith I give you and send those rocks rolling! Let torrential rains of healing crack them, use the wind of my Spirit to wipe off their faces, and funnel my redemptive fire through them. Watch them turn into a hollow shell that falls off your life. I am the God of all mountains, and those deceptive counterfeits are not from me! I am the God of mountains, wind, rain, and fire; I decide what makes a mountain!

What is too high a price? Parents, what won't you do for your baby? Labor pains, longer work hours, nothing is too much to keep your little one safe and carefree.

What is too high a price? Teachers, could your students it be? No money, limited funding yet through these hurdles you show them what they are meant to be.

What is too high a price? Soldier, what won't you do for your country? Family separation, war, nothing is too much to keep your country safe and free.

What is too high a price? Was it you? Was it me? God sent down His only Son and it was final. He refused to stop at anything until we would be free!

What is too high a price? Church, oh church, why do we grumble and think this way?! There is never too high a price we might pay to show a hopeless world the One who saves you and me!

The In Between

An in between, that infinitesimal moment after movement but before the action. A breathless second after the inhale but before the exhale. It's where nothing and a world of something all happen at once. It's where we live most of our lives.

In between growing up and growing old, we learn how to operate in this world but so often woefully neglect the spiritual realm. We are taught money, politics, work, and how to be good; but overlook God, Kingdom living, holy ethics, and how to be children of the King. But it's only for a moment, see, we are still in between.

In between loving this world and wishing for the next. We slave away in our daily routines while we dream of a perfect heaven to be. We hate our reality but love the earth. We love to talk of heaven and yet are terrified of death. We never truly learn to satisfy ourselves, instead we chafe against the discomfort of the in between.

In between learning to love and learning to hate is where we stake our ground. We hold dear ones close while shoving others away. We act as though one can't exist without the other, that in order to truly trust some we must despise others. In between here is where we lose friendships and gain enemies.

In between this fading world and the one coming, see, this is where we were created to be. Living where God's goodness is beginning to overwhelm earth, yet demons haven't fully fled. It is here where

He placed humanity in order to prove once and for all His honor reigns above all. This in between is where He placed His kids.

In between God and man is where Jesus stands. He balances God's judgment with His mercy. In this world both can't happen at once, but in God's Kingdom they are one and the same. Perfect judgment, perfect mercy, Jesus perfectly completed the requirements for each.

Now here is the real in between in this tussled, divided world caught between itself and the fast-approaching one of God. You see, we are in between here, in between two kingdoms and in between two lives. Now is the moment to make a choice, take a deep breath and decide; don't be caught in between True Life and the broken rules of this in between life.

"It is finished."

You gave up Your life for ours, and these were the last words You chose to say. But what is finished? So often it looks like evil will win. We see what appears to be death everywhere, fear widespread, physical and mental sickness continually spreading.

"It is finished." Darkness can no longer win. It is done, the outcome is set; evil has lost. Even though darkness still exists on earth, it has no hope of conquering. It is finished, beaten, no longer a threat.

"It is finished." Whispering voices in my head have lost their firm foothold. No longer allowed to speak endlessly, and I no longer need to listen. Though they at times still speak and lie; they are defeated, their ultimate end is coming.

"It is finished." Depression, bipolar, PTSD, and all the other acronyms and labels slapped on people. Those three words are their death knell, they have been routed. Their dwindling power slips from them daily.

"It is finished." Disease, viruses, illnesses with no names are on notice; the time of their demise creeps ever closer. The closer it gets, the more noises they make. Pay no attention to the panic they try to inflict, it's a last-ditch effort, the death gasps of a crumbling empire.

"It is finished." With this phrase, the cross You hung on became a bridge spanning the division of us to God. In that moment two kingdoms clashed together; the seen and the not yet visible now connected once again.

"It is finished." Not whispered words of a man dying, but the victory shout of the Son of Man entering the throne room of God with the very keys of death clenched in His hands. Though the battles still rage and at times look unwinnable, take heart Church, the outcome is set already; victory is imminent. The King of Kings has declared it and by His resurrection He proved it: "It is finished!"

You said, "Be joy." I heard "Make people laugh."

You said, "Be peace." I heard "Strive to be peaceful always."

You said, "Be patient."
I heard "Work at becoming a more patient person."

You said, "Be kind." I heard "Do good acts of kindness."

You said, "Be good."
I heard, "Always dig to find the good in others."

You said, "Be faithful."
I heard, "Your faith is built in your own strength."

You said, "Be gentle." I heard, "Let people run over me."

You said, "Be self-controlled."
I heard, "You are responsible for doing all this."

You said, "Be love."
I heard, "Kill yourself doing things for others. Prove your love."

Why do I always hear strive when all You said was be?
To be: To exist or live.
To do: to perform.

Church, why have so many of us become performers when all
God has ever asked is for us to live as His children?

Stop doing, just be.

Be His.

I Am that I Am
I am… the storm on the mountain
I am… the still small voice
I am… the Lord of angel armies
I am… the Father who gave His Son
I am… He who scatters His people
I am… the One who pulls them close
I am… Who you can't fully understand
I am all of these and more, but most importantly
I am totally in love with you.

You are… My highest creation
You are… My most excruciating loss
You are… the ones I made in My image
You are… My willfully disobedient children
You are… the reason I sent My son
You are… the ones who killed Him
You are… who I made to rule the earth
You are… the ones who gave away your crowns
You are… the ones I still choose
Regardless of past mistakes, future ones, or who you think you are
You are Mine

This was written just as we were to enter 30 days' isolation. Our church had just gathered for what was to be the last in-church service for 4 months but we didn't know that yet. We would emerge from that time changed but with the deep knowledge that God is for us.

Uncertainty, fear. It can be seen on people's faces, heard in their voices, posts, texts. The world is flaming up, blazing out in the grips of an unknown terror. Yet above it all, strumming like a heartbeat I hear You whisper, "I am for you."

The dread of the unknown. Friends and family who are more susceptible to this illness. Precautions are understandable for them; I get it and I agree. The self-isolation, however, feeds whispers of panic; yet they are silenced by Your voice, "I am for you!"

Economic failure, food shortages-desolation hangs in the air like a blanket feeding desperation. How does this end, is this the end? But the very real horror that is sitting in so many hearts is shaken loose by the sound of Your mighty roar, "I AM FOR YOU!"

"Don't be afraid, I am with you!" Your voice thunders the heavens, and I am shaken yet comforted. You are God, sovereign and holy! Regardless of what we hear being screamed by fear, You alone are in control. Terror, disease, death, these are not from You and will never succeed long term. You are for us!

> *"Don't be afraid, for I am with you. Don't be discouraged, for I am your God. I will strengthen you and help you. I will hold you up with my victorious right hand." Isaiah 41:10*

Cornerstone

Rocks, rocks everywhere tumbling around in my heart and head. They smack each other, cut grooves, but never actually break. Nothing seems to be able to break these rocks of mine; time doesn't erode them; in fact they only get denser and more defined. I want them to crack; I attack with a chisel, but as soon as I start to cut, they just compress a little stronger.

Rocks, rocks everywhere; they won't break so I just give up, shrug, and pretend not to care. I try to content myself with dragging them around forever. Just for fun I've even decided to give them names, Anger, Hurt, Unforgiveness, and this incredibly tough, large one that is my solidified heart. I walk with my load, each step harder than the last; my rocks are heavier than ever.

Rocks, rocks everywhere, and I swear they are growing. It's though they are fusing together, forming a large mega-boulder with my heart encased in the middle. This is too much to bear! I can't walk at all now and I barely breathe. Each inhale and exhale sends sharp pain through my body towards my chest. The pain never reaches my heart though, swallowed as it is. No one can live like this.

Rocks, rocks everywhere, they have won and I'm too busy trying not to die. This is it, my last breath… "God, I can't anymore, take whatever You can; I just want to live again." My wheezing exhale has become a prayer. The load lightens, but only a bit. I hear Your reply, "There is but one thing that can break these off. It's My Cornerstone. He can eradicate the rocks, but it will feel like He's destroying you, too." Destroy me too?! It sounds scary but I'm already being consumed. What more can Jesus do that I haven't already done to myself? "Do whatever it takes, I need to be free!"

Rocks, rocks everywhere and now I see the One that is going to break me free. He is sturdy, His hands reaching out not for my hands but my rocky mass. Grabbing hold of Anger He grips and twists. Craaack! Anger rips through the middle and falls off of me; the pain from my breathing seems deeper now like a little bit can touch my heart. Not content to let the Anger rock just stay on the ground, Jesus lifts a foot and stomps, grinding, stamping, and pulverizing it until dust remains. Oddly, each time He destroys a piece I still hurt, even though it's no longer attached.

Rocks, rocks everywhere; one is done but so many more remain. This doesn't bother the Cornerstone, He continues to rip, sever, and pulverize rocks attached to me. The pain is incredible, yet I can finally breathe again. With a thunderous yell from Him and pain-filled wail from me Unforgiveness is finally snapped off; only the jagged casing around my heart remains. This is enough, I can live again; my heart isn't truly free, but I'm not nearly as weighed down. Yes, I think I will forego the pain for now and just live with a few baby pebbles; they won't get big again, I'll keep an eye on them.

Rocks, rocks everywhere; there were so many but now only the last one remains. "You said, 'Do whatever it takes,'" God's tender voice reminds me. "I told you it would feel like this, will you trust Me now and let me break this last one? I promise the death you feel won't last." I whisper ok or maybe I simply nod, I'm completely shrouded in a haze of agony and terrified at the thought of death. Hands of granite swoop in one last time grabbing the shards trapping my heart. He hacks and slashes; it's too much, my heart is being ripped apart! Suddenly it's over; no more movement happens; I must be dead.

Chains of Freedom

Rocks, rocks nowhere to be seen; Jesus has stripped them all from me. In amazement, I gaze at the heart He now holds; soft, tender, and it's beating again! I finally see now; God was right in saying it would feel like death because He was bringing the dead back to life. My heart has feeling, spirit, and life again! But best of all Jesus, the one and only Cornerstone, holds it in His most capable hands. The Cornerstone that crushed my rocks and brought me back to life is now the One upon whom I live my life. I asked to be free, and it destroyed me; the Cornerstone broke me and then laid down a new foundation for me to build my life. One where He is the Rock that everything is now constructed on. Breaking on the Cornerstone is the only way I could live again; are you ready to die to live?

This storm has been rising for decades.

It's not over abortion or LGBTQ rights.

It holds no claim to blue or red states.

Black or blue lives don't matter to it either.

Pro-Ukraine or Pro-Russia sways it not; although our fear of nukes excites it.

These are all rumbles and flashes but they aren't the storm itself; they are the after-affects that we can see and feel.

The storm is deeper still.

You know it's true, you can feel it too; the churning, twisting feeling in your gut.

That thing that catches in your throat late at night when you ponder what ifs.

The ache for yesteryear every time you think of tomorrow.

This storm is a battle for the soul; not of a country but the Church.

It's forcing us to decide who we are and Whose we are.

Too long we have walked this line between following God and placating others.

We thought a little nap here or there wouldn't cost us anything.

We didn't really need to be on the lookout all the time.

We used pretty Christianese words, called it "being everything to everyone," when in reality we were just falling in love with our sin.

Oh, we caught a lightening flash or two and occasionally we stirred ourselves to half-wake claiming that the Spirit will make up what we lack.

This was just to make sure we didn't ever have to fully commit to one side or the other; the tightrope we loved to walk and slip on.

But now the storm is here, now half-hearted platitudes won't cut back the wind.

The flashes of lightening only expose our emptied watchtowers.
Thunder rumbles and drowns out our pitiful, half-conscious yells.
No more can we keep shooting our arrows at movements, unbelievers, and so incredibly often, each other.
The time of platitudes and tightrope walking is over; we must claim a side or die in indecision.
The storm is rolling in.

Wake up now Church or perish like so many did in 70 AD clinging to a temple God had deserted.

Ultimate Love

The man and woman hid in the forest terrified of the anger headed towards them. They had only one command to follow and they broke it. "Don't eat the fruit from that tree, or you will die." Such a simple thing to adhere to. In a garden filled with other foods, why was that one even attractive? But they had tried it. Willingly deceived by the very creature they ruled over, they touched the fruit then bit down. I wonder how long it took before they began to regret their decision. One bite? The whole fruit, or maybe just a single chew? No matter when it happened, regret and shame did set in. So did fear; so they hid, away from God, away from the wrath and death they were sure was headed their way.

But what came was so much worse. No anger or wrathful punishment. Instead they could hear the wail of God crying out, "Where are you? What have you done?" The groan of a Father who had just been separated from His children. And the agony of knowing they had unwittingly severed the whole point of living from their lives. It was probably at this point when they realized they had died; the part of their soul that was intimately connected with God had been cut off. It wasn't immediate, but now their bodies and souls were indeed dying.

We so quickly judge the actions of Adam and Eve, yet we never think about the awfulness of having to live for hundreds of years after their one action changed everything. Tilling the land, the pain of childbirth, these were nothing compared to the realization of never being able to dwell face to face with God again. How excruciating to live day after day without God's intimate presence. And yet God was already moving towards reconciliation. In His great love, He withdrew the fullness of His splendor in order to not destroy humanity with His complete glory. He began His plan of redemption, thousands of years of restoring a family, a people, and a country to Himself. Culminating with sending a piece of Himself, Jesus, to earth to save us from the sin that still grows within us.

He did all this to reset a single sin. We so often fear the wrath of God that we never notice He hasn't acted in anger towards us, but He has literally created a new way to be face to face with Him again. These aren't the actions of a God who damns people, but the God who will do literally everything to love you. One fruit, two silly people, and the whole world went into darkness; one God responded in love so deep that He wrote Himself into our history. If He did all this for one single sin, then no one is out of His reach to save. Not me and not you.

The Garden

As You bend Your face to us once again may we be pleasing to You. Hear our praises, our joyous proclamations of Your beauty and might. May it be lovely to Your ears and a perfume of luxurious incense delightful to You.

As You bend Your face to us once again may we be pleasing to You. We are your people, planted in Your greenhouse. Let our lives be an everlasting testament to You. Come walk through the garden of Your people again! See the beauty You created laid down in honor and surrender to You. We are your people; come see the gloriously lush orchard You have planted.

As You bend Your face to us once again may we be pleasing to You. Your garden and orchards cry out for more of You. As a flower's fragrance pleases the gardener may our perfume of prayer and worship be ever pleasing to You, God of all creation! Do not withhold Your waters from our thirsty souls, Father, we must have Your rainy flood to live!

As You bend Your face to us once again may we be pleasing to You. Almighty Caretaker, cut, prune, and shear away what must die. We might wince from that pain of pruning but I would rather be cut off from the rot that would kill my heart. Remove all disease from our branches that we may be overflowing in ripe fruit to give the lost, hungry world.

As You bend Your face to us once again may we be pleasing to You. Bountiful, vibrant, a balm of perfume; a garden of Your people wholly pleasing to You alone. Come walk among Your

people once again, be enthroned upon our praises, and revive us
once again.

A new wind is blowing, can you hear it?

But this is no soft breeze that gently tousles the hair and goes away leaving the area unchanged.

A cyclone is coming intent on tearing down religious factions and divisions, nothing will remain standing.

What will you do when revival gusts blast?

I am determined to be caught up, tossed in the air, and let the gale dash any hypocrisy away.

A storm is coming, can you feel it?

The thunder rumbles and vibrates through our souls.

We prayed for the lightning and fire of God's Spirit and He is sending them.

Will you continue to hide away in your buildings where spiritual decay and death already knocks at the door?

I will not! Let the thunder rumble, let the lightning strike, burn away all of me until only He remains.

The rain is coming, can you smell it?

A fresh scent wafts ever closer; taste the drops about to fall.

The first drops are hitting, I can hear dry ground being sprinkled; now a gushing downpour drenching everything, the floodwaters are rising.

Will you run away from the tidal waves; where could you hide that revival currents cannot reach?

Look, out in the flood that's where I'll be; I'm going to dance in revival rain.

We can hear it, feel it, and smell it; revival is coming, but will we be ready when it gets here?

Warrior Women

Arise, O mighty lioness! Awaken once again to the sound of battle. Warrior women, who heed the call of heaven, ready to charge at a moment's notice. The world is in dire need of women who march to Jehovah's heart, who can tear down a stronghold and also soothe a wounded heart. Society cries out for women with the character of Deborah; judges who can lead with a balanced and firm hand not hesitating to fight the spiritual enemies who seek to destroy. The legacy of Deborah still echoes; she led her people to total freedom from all oppressors.

Arise, O mighty lioness! Can you not hear the sound of destruction rumbling in the distance? It can be stopped, it takes the hearts of mighty women like Moses' mother to do it. Not even named, yet her courage changed everything for the Israelites. It was hard to hide a baby and then send him down the river, but how heartbreaking to care for him everyday and not get to be his full mother! Not all battles are hand fought, many are done in private; many times by unnamed, unsung heroes. Yet she did it and because of her sacrifice the slaves were freed and an entire nation was reconciled to God. To this day, Israel still holds the same land that was promised to Moses.

Arise, O mighty lioness! Look around, see the unseen evil and fight it in God's way. Sometimes, evil is at the door and there is nowhere to run. Combat it like Rahab, she saw her own city and people were going to be demolished by the Israelites. Unlike everyone else, she sought the help of an unknown God. Jehovah, who overlooked the fact that she wasn't Jewish and even worse was a prostitute. Her fighting was by way of hospitality to spies. She saved her entire family from death and now her bloodline is Jewish. God is raising warrior women amongst all races, ; backgrounds and pasts will not stop His willingness.

Arise, O mighty lioness! How many more stories of old need to be told? Feel that rising heat in your chest, see your eyes lighting up; this is the call to fight! It's time to stand and get in formation. Not to make another march, argue in another social media post; it's time to rescue the babies in baskets, give firm and Godly counsel, and war for our families! This is the goal of true Christianity, not to have a nice church service, but to pray, pound the ground, intercede, and worship until the battle is won. Our place is to be the physical representation of a God who loves us enough to fight for us. Our battles might be in the mundane of life but we never know whose future that changes. The call for action is sounding now. Are there warrior women ready to answer?

I see the effects of Your design in every seed that blooms.

Every star that shoots across the universe proves Your touch continues to create.

The wild variations of Your creativity are evident in every creature that roams, soars, swims, and climbs.

Throughout creation, proof of Your handiwork sings of the God you are.

I feel Your Presence in the joyful smile of a 2-year-old as he yells, "Bye, I love you," at bedtime.

I sense Your strength in the slightly shaky confidence of friends who are stepping forward into new futures.

I hear Your joy in the voice of a family member who is embracing sobriety and Your peace springs forth from my brother as he sings Your praises.

I see Your freedom whenever I look in the mirror and the face of resurrected life stares back at me.

I see the effects of You in every piece of creation but it is only in Your created humanity that I see Your Presence actively working.

Sold, but left along the road abandoned.

That was me before Jesus.

Sold to rebellion, alcohol, rage, hatred, lust-anything that felt good at the time.

But like a good party and a wild night, I would be left alone in the aftermath.

An afterthought, a mess that they didn't want to clean up.

Sold but not claimed, only temporarily used.

Each encounter only scuffed, ripped holes, and pulled at my seams.

Labels placed over the torn areas like band-aids; addict, PTSD, bipolar, lesbian.

They provided momentary relief but only covered the wounds so they remained open and raw.

I settled in for a life of brokenness.

And then I saw Him again for the first time in decades.

As He drew near, I shrank back, afraid He would see my wounds and ugly torn places.

Then I saw His; lash marks on His back, holes in His arms and feet, a gash in His side.

No labels to cover them, no handmade bandages, yet they were healed.

And His sign, so similar to mine and yet eternally different.

"Sold- for you, for your healing. Sold, my death for your life."

"Do not be afraid, for I have ransomed you. I have called you by name; you are mine." Isaiah 43:1b

Chains of Freedom

I'm the God who speaks and the dead are raised.
I AM Healing.
I'm the God who spits on dirt and heals the blind.
I AM Healing.
I'm the God who told a man to dip in a dirty river to cure leprosy.
I AM Healing.
I'm the God who uses people to heal others.
I AM Healing.

Your wounds do not confound me.
I AM Healing.
Your trauma does not overwhelm me.
I AM Healing.
Your diagnosis cannot stop me.
I AM Healing.
Your sickness will not overcome me.
I AM Healing.

I see you, regardless of every hurt, sickness, trauma, and diagnosis.
    I see the creation I made.
I know your name; not the lies who whisper or the illness who
    calls you broken. I know your true name.
I AM your Father and healing is my nature.
I AM Jehovah Rapha thundering from the heavens, coming to
    you!

You've touched me and I'm forever ruined. Nothing else can satisfy and like an addict I crave more and more of You.

I'm ruined, Your love has flooded my soul. Reaching in and touching the hidden places; the dark bruises I tried to forget about. Love so wild that it dares to speak my wholeness.

I'm wrecked by Your passion. Dreams awaken in me again. I hear Your voice speaking and guiding, creating desires in me.

I am free from the lies, whispers, and chains. I am wrecked, ruined, and finally free to be who You created.

Revival has destroyed me back to life.

Thoughts of You

When I think of You, I think of life. Never-ending, vibrant, creative life. You spoke a word and galaxies formed. A lifeless earth sprang into being with animals, vegetation, and waters. Your creativity knows no limits. You have never replicated a sunset or sunrise exactly the same, yet they happen daily.

You breathed, and man came alive in Your image.

When I think of You, I think of glory. Not mine, yours. Who can contend with the God whose very presence can kill from the glory of His face?! Your glory covers the earth, causes mountains to quake, and oceans to split; yet you place it over me with gentle care.

Glory that has killed men and yet a child can stand it.

When I think of You, I think of honor. The honor of being Your child and also giving You honor. My King and my Abba; two in one, a double honor portion fit for my Jehovah-Provider.

My life is to live for Your honor, my joy is continual praise to You.

Jesus, Coffee, and Therapy

A few months into my new life with God I had a massive mental breakdown. I couldn't understand what was happening or why I was losing my mind when I had finally found it with Jesus. For the next 8 months to a year, I walked through a valley of realizing the mess I was, that trauma must come out to be released, and that our God walks every step of it with us when we let Him. I learned that healing can be instant, or it can come gradually in the form of therapy and medication. These were hard days, but I now know with absolute certainty that God will never, ever leave me in the valley.

I asked You to call me out to deeper waters. You answered with a question, "What if I ask you to come down to the depths of your trauma? Past the horror, past the anguish, to the very root of the pain. Would you still ask for the deeper waters?"

I'm not so casual to respond. Part of me wants to scream and refuse, another wants to cower and hide away. Away from the memories that begin to surface with just a whisper of trauma; hide, hide, hide all the baggage and try desperately to forget it's there.

The smallest part of me, just a sliver really, quietly says, "Yes, I still ask." This is me, the real me, the one desperate enough to do the impossible. The me that is growing in courage and faith. I'm desperate not only to make the pain end but totally desperate for You.

You aren't asking me to relive all the awfulness because I deserve to but because it's the only way for it to go away once and for all. It's ugly and some days will be hard and others even worse, yet You are with me every breath of the way.

You aren't promising I'll forget but that I will finally remember without flinching, without memories driving in like arrows. I realize now that at the bottom of all this mess is where I find freedom and where the trauma truly dies.

"Go back to the beginning." Not a phrase I like to hear directed at me. The beginning of what? I can go back for a while, but then it gets all muddled and I don't know if I'm at the beginning, middle, end, or a galaxy far away. Yet You are asking me to go back, so away I will go.

Suddenly all my past misdeeds come zooming into focus, bad decisions, even worse actions, and a trail of heartache are all immediately front and center. While not exactly what I had hoped for, this is at least familiar territory. Still I'm not sure of what I'm looking for, the beginning I guess. "This isn't the beginning, go back farther," I hear You say.

Next up on this train ride to The Beginning features lies I believed about me. Hundreds of lies, some I was told by others and sadly, even more ones I told to myself. Whispers of terrible half-truths, evil full truths twisted in hate, and a few beautiful but hugely wrong ones. I don't like this place. It's still a spot I sometimes fall into, and I almost always get lost here. I want to leave. "This isn't the beginning either, go back farther."

Zip! Off we go but to where I don't know. We are now hitting territory too hazy to fully remember. Suddenly with perfect clarity I see it: The Beginning. At least the one I can remember, anything farther is too young. But there it is; the moment I began to believe the lie. A young girl being mocked by other kids, laughed at and called fatherless. There it is, the lie-fatherless. It wound its way tightly into my soul so deep that even though I now have a good earthly father, I always secretly wondered if he would leave. This

sick game doesn't continue long because another child puts a stop to it.

"Go back to the beginning." I'm here now and it's as sucky as it was when I was little, but I don't see anything wildly different. In fact, I don't see You at all. This realization smacks as hard as the fact that I am just noticing that I'm angry at You about all this. Where were You, all those years ago?! Weren't You there in the beginning?! "Look again." The scene repeats itself and I can barely stand to watch it again. But something seems a little different this time, I can't tell what. In comes the little girl who stops the others and, then that is when I see the difference. You are there! Coming out of her eyes as she sees me. Speaking out of her mouth as she tells the others to stop. You were there all along. I was never alone, not even in the beginning.

Bumps in the road. Some are deeper than others, it looks like a little one except this hole goes down 6 inches. My body tenses for impact but not from the pothole; instead I see riot grenades, rocks filled with screws and nails, and flaming oranges flying all around. I know one is going to get me sometime, will it be today? Whew, I guess not...Whack, one rock to the helmet, one to the chest. Suck it up, tomorrow is another fight to survive.

Bumps in the road. They look simple, just a little elevation and a jostle. But to me they are a slap, a human bomb exploding in the seat next me. Will I accidentally drive off the road? Maybe into oncoming traffic-this thought isn't a reflection as much as a sad wish. But no, this time I drive on with just another smack.

Bumps in the road. This one is a road wide trench, it's deep and there is no way around it. I'm not even in my car any more, this pounding thud has sent me to an old hell that I thought I had escaped. Words dripping with hate are the nicest part of my days. The worst are electric cords, flying household items, and broom sticks. Part of me wants to escape, part of me keeps saying I deserve this; all of me just wants this to be over, just end it already.

Bumps in the road. I know that's what they are, but someone forgot to tell my body about them. The dip, bump, jostle and I'm in another world completely. And I never get to choose which one, sometimes it's Iraq, others it's my ex. Occasionally it's a very weird mixture of both. But I know it's a bump that's plain as day, it's where the bump sends me that is terrifying.

Bumps in the road. Iraq, domestic hell, and a host of other crashes and thumps along the way; they are just bumps. Someday I'll hit a pothole with glee because someday the bumps won't be able to affect me. Just like the very real bumps in the road, they were in my life, then in my rearview mirror, and finally invisible, gone past eyesight never to knock me again.

Body Memories

How long does the body remember? A book dropped, foot stomp, or a simple hand near me and I'm lost. My brain struggles to remember where it is. I don't usually get totally lost in my mind anymore. Rather it's like I see two wildly different pictures competing to see which one will win out. Luckily reality does most of the time. But my body is a different story. The more my mind spits out, the more my body recalls. Every boom, shaking, jarring, each violent action sets my body on edge. It still reacts the same way it did years ago with a flinch and every nerve screaming to the point of shutdown. It's like all my nerve receptors flare with painful overstimulation and then nothing. My brain turns the switch, and I suddenly feel numb to any touch. When does this period end?

How long does Your body remember? Does metal striking metal or a high-pitched whistle cause You to flinch? I know Your mind has no fear of the past, but Your body is similar to ours so maybe it still remembers, even if only slightly. Though You have no fear of pain or memories, I believe You still remember every moment of Your crucifixion. You paid the highest price for us and You won't forget it. But neither will You be held by the flashes and memories of the worst day in creation. Even if the occasional flinch still twitches, You are never overwhelmed with memories.

I cling to the hope of that day for me, where the noise, memory, or smell causes nothing more than a simple twinge of remembrance then nothing, and my day continues. It will happen, I know it will and so I don't give up. I take the ever increasing good days and celebrate the simple milestones, like driving myself to the gym, with joyful thanks for Your healing and restoration. The hard days I choose to view as good days with speed bumps that are ever decreasing in power and potency. Those days have an expiration date, so until then I rest in the knowledge that You truly understand dark memories. And I have hope that mine will someday change lives; after all, Your darkest day saved the world.

Too Far

You almost had me until I remembered how much I can't stand bullies. I've never been one to look the other way when someone is being picked on. I'm not about to let you pick on me anymore. I don't allow others to be demeaned or disrespected and I'm not about to let you intimidate me any longer! Bullies never know when to quit; they poke and poke until their victim attacks back. Their pride just won't let them quit until they inevitably try their methods on the wrong kid.

You almost had me when you slyly slipped in digs like, "How old are you now? What kind of loser reinvents their life at 34? God won't take you anyhow." I started to believe you until I remembered Noah was over 100, Abraham was 90+, and Moses was 80 when he said, "Let my people go." According to those ages, my great strides with God won't begin for another 40 years or so! Let's not forget the most important one, Jesus was 33 when He died but after that He hasn't stopped working since.

You almost had me; I was down and ready to tap out. But you just couldn't stop yourself; you had to throw in one more whisper, "This will never end, give up, die." That last word was one too many. I've fought too hard and long to be alive again; asking me to quit was that last push. Besides, I've almost died many times before, and yet I still live; how dare you think you can change what God Almighty has done?

Satan, you almost had me until you just didn't quit. I was down, crippled, in a fog, but you had to kick one last time. That kick was one too many; it did what I couldn't do for myself. It woke me up.

Congratulations devil, you woke the warrior in me back up. Now she is shaking off her stupor, picking up her armor and sword, ready to climb back up to her place on the wall. Because you're too proud to know when to stop, I'm now alert, vigilant, and conscious of your ways. Thanks for that last boot; you're proving yet again how the Kingdom of God will advance even through your tactics!

I see you. That night where drunk you met someone who took advantage. I see you the next morning scurrying around to hide a night you want to erase but can't ever forget.

I see you. Surrounded by violence, learning to revel in it, to become one with hate. I see you, laughing at others' agony, unaware and unconcerned that your soul cries in agony too.

I see you. Addiction has chained you down, you don't even remember the last time you were sober. I see you, drinking, collapsing, secretly hoping this is the night you don't wake up.

I see you. Your "dream" relationship is a nightmare, every day is a new wave of where to get hit next. I see you; you won't even fight back anymore, the voices in your head tell you it's your fault and you believe them.

I see you. The end is rapidly spinning towards you; two days in the summer heat, pills, and alcohol. I see you; this is what you want, not death maybe but an end, a stop to the cycle of violence, insanity, and pain. I'm crying for you to listen and see Me.

I see you. Broken yet guarded, you won't trust the words you hear about My forgiveness but you want to. I see you, your hurt and heart, the tendrils of trust reaching out to see if I will still accept you.

I SEE YOU! I've been waiting for this day since the dawn of eternity. "I SEE YOU!" I am thundering from the heavens; my child, my princess, my daughter is back in My arms. We are together again, this is what I have been waiting for since the dawn of time. I see you, and now you finally see Me too!

Random Head Conversations

"Don't fight, just fall back into your slumber. God will understand if you can't stand anymore, He should still love you." Your words are soothing but not comforting, I don't remember any point where God told us to sleep. And what do you mean by He should still love me? I recall somewhere in the Bible, He said He had cherished me since before my birth, before the foundations of earth even.

"So your progress slipped a little today. It's okay, God doesn't expect you to overcome every time, He understands that you can't always stand in Him." It's nice to know that no progress doesn't mean failure, wait did you just say that I'm not an overcomer? But God has called me more than an overcomer, and above all to stand. Who exactly am I talking to?

"But you're different, He was telling the apostles and 'real' Christians those things. You aren't being physically persecuted so it really doesn't pertain to you. God really just expects you to live a good life, don't make waves." Hold up, now I know you aren't telling me any of God's truth! Jesus said because I believe in Him, I can do even more than He did. Physical persecution isn't the only form and you have tormented my head long enough. I know these swirly thoughts and I know they aren't from God or me.

So here is some truth for you, fallen one; you roar like a lion but I am protected by the Lion of Judah! Do I stumble and even fall at times? Sure, but the Great Shepherd is there ready to help me back up and extend brand new mercies daily. And another thing I know, you are a disgraced angel only, not a god and not on equal footing with my Father, the King of kings. When He speaks you must listen and obey him. You said you would ascend above God but you can't; to top it off, He has given us authority to use His name against you! In hindsight, maybe you should have just skipped over trying to screw with my head this morning.

You probably never knew my name. In fact, I'm positive you didn't because you're not the type of person to hurt little kids. But you did, when you whispered lies about my parents behind their backs telling others they weren't to be trusted. "That new pastor and his wife don't seem right, they're too churchy, always talking about revival." You didn't talk about me but I saw and heard you. You weren't trying to teach but I understood your lesson, church people should never be trusted. Maybe you don't recall or maybe you do; but today I choose to forgive you.

You might not remember me; I dimly recall you. Your physical details escape me, but what you did physically hasn't faded even after 15 years. I was drunk, you probably were too but apparently not drunk enough to forget to slink away after you stole something precious. Maybe you don't recall or maybe you do; but today I choose to forgive you.

My first day at work, you tried to light me on fire. Your hatred ran so deep that you took every chance possible to spit on me, throw things at me, and even tried to kill me. I learned how to despise you, to be the infidel that you called me. You labeled me a monster and I became all that and more. We debased each other while claiming to be the better man; yet murder tastes the same in every language. You killed some of my friends and I maimed some of yours. Maybe you don't recall or maybe you do; but today I choose to forgive you.

We were supposed to be together forever, you and me. It wasn't too long before I realized forever was a seemingly never-ending

Chains of Freedom

cycle of pain. We both made terrible choices I'll agree, I stole and lied while you cut me down verbally and used your fists. "Chosen love" had placed us together in an abusive cycle bound to last forever or until one of us died. And I almost did. Maybe you don't recall or maybe you do; but today I choose to forgive you.

I don't feel like forgiving you, but forgiveness isn't a feeling, it's a choice. It's the choice to see all the sick both yours and mine too and allow God to suck the poison out. No, the memory isn't gone, it doesn't magically disappear. But God can remove the pain, torment, and anguish associated with them. So, I don't force myself to feel some odd emotion that I need to work myself into. I simply decide that regardless of how I feel, good or bad, I choose forgiveness. That is why today I choose to forgive you.

We probably won't be friends, but I no longer hold you captive in my heart. You're free to go, released from a cage you didn't know you were in. I do this for you, yes, but mostly for me. Choosing to set you free is my way of forgiving me. By harboring ill towards you, I'm only binding me. This is God's way of truly setting me free. So maybe you don't recall or maybe you do; but today when I forgive you, I forgive me too.

Wounded No More

I know you feel like you're still her; the little girl who might lose her father's love. That arrow struck deep and then snapped. The arrowhead stayed fast and over time flesh regrew over it. But it never healed just festered, calloused, and festered some more. Even when your father never left, you still secretly fretted. Even when I never left, in fear you turned and walked away.

I know you feel like you're still her - the warrior who didn't fulfill her duties. The broken exhaustion that stole your career took more than a job. Misplaced as it was, your identity was snatched along with your place in life. That arrow took you out at the knees, pulled you down and left you crippled. How many years will you be content to crawl along?

I know you feel like you're still her - the old yet newbie in this walk with Me. You're so excited to learn, yet terrified that you still might not qualify. Arrows still keep flying at you, but you're figuring out how to wear the armor I've given you. I see you put it on and still wonder if it's really for you. And you're realizing that the arrows still stuck inside you hurt even more when you wear it. I watch as you confusedly put it on and then take it off over and over again.

Finally you're ready; you've decided regardless of who you feel like, you're going to take Me at My word. With great joy I now begin to remove your arrows and heal! Don't fight me, don't pull away, your past shame will be no more! Tenderly I pluck that arrow in your heart; let the sting bite for a second and feel the salve of My healing pour over you. No more will you pull back from love and feeling; from this point on it will be your trademark. I am your loving Father and we are fully united again!

Next I help you stand again, out pops the other arrow; My children never have to crawl or grovel! Feet unsteady, I beam with happiness as you begin to walk, each step becoming more solid, more sure. Now you're ready; notice now each piece of My armor was made fitted perfectly for you. Wear it daily and no more arrows can pierce into you. Now you're My daughter-warrior; covered in My armor and healed from the inside out. Your head no longer hangs in shame, your passion-filled eyes pierce to the heart of people. Those who see you know you are truly your Father's daughter; filled with love and ready to battle for those wounded like you were.

The Staircase

I have a stairway inside me. The end is deep within me, nestled where my hopes and dreams used to reside. I haven't been down there in a very long time; I wonder if I even know where it'll end. Will there still be any down there or will I hit the last stop and fall off? A Voice answers my unspoken question with a question, "Are you willing to take the journey with Me and see what is down there?" To find the answer on this journey I now go.

1, 2, 3…9 steps down, so far so good. This isn't so bad in fact it's kind of easy. All the steps seem solid, nothing too worn, the handrail sturdy. It's pretty light here, a few shadows in corners but nothing too bad. In fact I see beautiful things written on the walls, Scriptures, poems, and letters all bright and colorful. I like my descent thus far.

10, 11, 12…21 Whoa, someone turned off the light! I can't see a thing, I grip onto the handrail confused; which way is up and which is down? This darkness is thick, tangible, like something alive. My brain begins to hear things, whispers, voices that speak terrible things. "You're a failure, you're bound to die, you can never escape who you were!" Terrified, I cover my ears and cower, but then the Voice reminds me, "You are mine, I have conquered for you, just keep walking." A light surrounds me, peaceful and soothing chasing the darkness and voices away. After a breath, I journey on.

22, 23, 24….35, I am getting so tired! How many more steps are there? I have already stopped twice for breaks and I can barely continue. Trying to get my mind off the stairs, I look around.

Chains of Freedom

These steps aren't empty, laying on them are items discarded and worn by time and neglect. A toy gun from when I used to pretend to be Jesse James, old army camo pants that reminded me of summers playing war in the woods. I see them and remember all the memories coupled with all the older girls telling me that I shouldn't do boy stuff, that it was unnatural. Riiiip, the pants seam opened up and the gun fell down another stair. I get it now, this is where the toys and clothes of my childhood clashed with weird social and "religious" expectations creating an identity that was never supposed to be mine. Sad at the thought of how long I believed these untruths, I stop for a quick breath and continue on.

36, 37,38, the steps continued on and on, each new set showing me parts of me coupled with parts of society's unrelenting constraints on me. This is heartbreaking, I don't want to continue but I must. The gentle light ever around me, ever comforting and soothing. 48, 49, 50! My foot hits the bottom floor and the sound echoes. It's silent here and apparently by the sound of the continuing reverberations it's empty too. Angrily, I yell out to the Voice in the light, "I walked down all the stupid steps just to see it's empty?! Why would you have me do this?!"

"I asked you to travel with Me so I could show you this!" Suddenly brilliant light floods the area and for a moment I'm blinded, unable to see anything. I gasp and look around, shelves upon shelves line the walls. This isn't any empty room at all, it's chock full! Items fill the shelves, my camo pants neatly sewn, my toy gun dusted and put up. Item after item from childhood to adult, a Happy Birthday Barbie, a pair of awful pink shades, my first BB gun, Rollerblades, it never ends. "Look at the walls," says the Voice. They are filled with words, wonderful, beautiful, life-giving words about me. "This is what you needed to see. You wondered if there was anything down here; I am. You invited Me in and I took the very deepest part of you restored, redeemed, and renovated it. You are no longer who society, "religion," or doctors say; you are mine and I say you are everything you were ever meant to be!"

So this is where my staircase ends, not in broken dreams or dashed hopes but in the Savior-King who redeems everything. My staircase no longer has broken, dark, or scary spots but it took a journey of faith; a step into the dark to fix it. There are no more shadowy voices or broken toys but this does

require an upkeep. I walk the staircase regularly now to make sure no clutter invites itself back in. This is a walkway I keep clear because I desire clarity and a good connection with my Father. Everyone has a staircase, when was the last time you traveled yours?

Identity Lost, Identity Found

At birth we set out to figure out our identity. Some of us slip right into the roles we were meant for; so many others try role after role with little to no success. What we don't know is our identity was birthed in us, our very first breaths were exclamations of our Godly identity. Every role we try on our own is actually a lie designed to steal us away from our specific calling. Every childhood incident, neighborhood bully, hateful word spoken to us, or a plethora of other things begins to work against the very identity God planted in us.

Tomboy, chatterbox, too athletic, and unfeminine; all just words that were flung around, but they caught hold in my mind and heart. Tomboy, apparently this was only ok until puberty, then I became an oddity amongst my female friends. Chatterbox, this one can't be helped, everyone in my family talks a lot, but I have actually been told that it's not nice to appear too much smarter than boys. Too athletic, hooboy, this was a hard one! Boys really don't like it when girls are a lot better than them at sports; again I was cautioned to play "nicer." Unfeminine, this was scarier to people, even more so than tomboyish; this meant I was apparently now actively against my sex. Not only did these words begin to define me, so did experiences. Partying, wanton violence, blackouts, these all re-enforced what I thought I was: worthless, useless.

With age, the names and experiences changed, but the meanings were pretty much the same until they morphed into one word, one new identity that I could claim-lesbian. The words and experiences swirling around me settled into this new identity that I got to choose, that no one could take away, and I could throw at other people like a wall stopping them before they had the chance to hurt me. It's no wonder that around the time I came out, I began to recoil from physical affection. Hugs from people other than immediate family and whoever I was dating at the time ceased. My walls were high and I thought I was unreachable from the harsh words I used to hear. But I was wrong; the walls I made were literally created with the same words designed to hurt me. Now I not only heard them daily, I said them to myself; I made the very things that cut me into my identity.

I'm not alone, I'm not unique; everyone has words, incidents, events, that shape them. Some of these things are huge and some are so small you probably can't even remember why you began to think of yourself negatively. From birth we are inundated with experiences, conversations, outside factors that the enemy actively uses to try and shape our identity away from God. Every single person has believed lies about themselves, but we don't have to continue to accept these foreign identities. God is continually calling us back to be the child He created, to use the identity we have in Him. We are heirs of the mightiest King! We are each called to do the works of our Father and walk as Jesus walked. We are royalty, yet so often we throw down our crowns and sit on the corner to beg like paupers. Don't make the enemy's job easy; pick up your crown and head back into battle! With our true identity we cannot lose. God's children are winners and always victorious.

When those things try to whisper at you, shout back the goodness of God. Instead of listening to worthless and useless scream in my head, I remind myself that God knew me from before the beginning of time; He was so excited about my life before the earth was created, it's not possible for me to be worthless. He calls me part of the body of Christ where each person has roles and duties; therefore I am not useless. Whatever satan would raise before you as a way to cripple you, demolish that lie with the very words of

God! Our God is good and in Him no darkness can live; let's wrap ourselves so deep into God's identity that no power of hell can get anywhere near us. Church, let's be who we were always meant to be, united in God, conquerors through Christ, and utterly unstoppable!

When I first heard Your song, I couldn't answer it. Years of bondage and captivity chained my tongue in silence. The closest I could get was to speak Your name as a curse. And then You came and blasted through the shackles!

You sang a song of freedom into my soul and I was raised to life.

Finally, I could sing with You!

But what came out was a primal wail; powerful and longing to speak the truth but filled with bitter brokenness. Still You sang, each chorus soothing the jagged pieces of me. As You continued, I kept mumbling along until finally the sick bitter root popped out of my spirit.

Over and over, You kept singing, teaching me Your words.

What I thought were cracks and flaws in my voice were areas where You were breathing new lyrics of Your character into me. Finally, I realized You were teaching me how to sing Your words to others, they aren't to be kept to myself.

Your song of deliverance over me is what I now sing over others. The words You used to heal me, I now use to give healing to others. I am learning to harmonize my whole life with You.

Once a captive, I am now free to set others free.

Listen. Can you hear it?

"No justice, no peace!" Political parties being bantered around like gang affiliations.

Beneath the roar of angry words and violence demanding justice, there is a generation calling for real peace. They are asking to know what true justice is, crying out for someone to teach them live in true unity.

Listen. Do you hear it?

"Change your name, gender, just be whatever you feel."

Beyond the clamor of so many labels defining people, there is a fatherless generation crying for an identity. They beg to know that there is a spiritual inheritance, a place, and a true family for them.

Listen. The whisper is becoming a roar impossible to ignore.

"Truth is relative, it's only important if it's my truth." They scream for truth; your truth, my truth, which one is right? Everything is suspect.

Below the cries of misguided truths is a generation who screams for an absolute. They are yearning to know legitimate Truth. Jesus, the God-man who came from Heaven; He is absolute God and absolute Truth all wrapped in one.

How many beautiful songs do we have about hearing the cries of a generation? But are we listening? Can we really hear their wails? I fear too often we find ourselves focusing on their words but failing to catch the groans and sobs sitting below the surface.

Listen to the cries of a generation.

"Let me see through you that there is more to life; prove to me that my life matters. Teach me, show me real justice and peace! Give me a Father and an identity! Take me to Truth and tell me His name!"

A flash of skin grabs the eyes, but it's the soul that crumbles in shame.

Only a single moment but it seems like nothing will ever be the same.

Shame, guilt, and loathing don't give up their prey easily.

Even when Freedom beckons; they whisper, "Pray all you want but you'll never be unshackled."

I close my eyes and see all the things I don't want to see.

Glimpses, bursts of images; I know I'm forgiven but shame doesn't seem to let go.

An unwanted companion who reminds me that some innocence isn't restorable.

How can an heir to the King live with such a vile mess?

The One who has proven He forgives offers, "Come see this from My view."

I see myself and that awful, messy, thing- shame. It's swirling, engulfing me just as I knew it would.

"Look closer." Now I see them, the painful chains that rattle my head. But they aren't connected to me.

I'm… I'm holding them. I've been free the whole time.

Shame just had me convinced I was still chained.

Rock bottom.

Such a strange sounding term and for many people it's a place they desperately try to avoid. But we all hit rock bottom at some time. Most of us hit it more than once. There is a strange beauty in being at rock bottom.

Everything is exposed, no more secrets, no more desperately trying to hide the mess anymore.

It's here at the end of things where we can finally see that the shame we've been dragging around was never ours to keep. The victimization, addiction, and brokenness were not meant for us to carry.

The guilt came because we thought those things were who we were, rather than what happened to us.

Rock bottom forces us to look up and see the lies that were whispered, screamed, and beat into our head.

Rock bottom allows us to release the pressure of perfection and lets us be imperfectly human.

Rock bottom strips away the last vestiges of useless pride and replaces it with a humility that can withstand a thousand storms.

If we look, we will see that rock bottom is a promise of a new beginning. Not a redirection but a changing of courses.

The true beauty in absolute bottom comes when we realize that in that awful moment, that pain-filled time of brokenness, we are not alone.

It is here, in the utter lowest depths; when our pride is gone, and we are defenseless that God yearns to meet us.

Not to judge but to love.

Not to tear down but to rebuild.

It is here at rock bottom where God met me and replaced my broken rock bottom with Jesus, the only true Cornerstone.

"Dare to dream again."

These words dropped into my spirit with such force during worship. But what did they mean? I'm a dreamer by nature, a big thinker type who is constantly coming up with ideas. I'm almost always dreaming, so what could it mean by "dream again?"

Lately I feel like I've been_dreaming more than ever. Thinking about what the future might hold, coming up with plan A, B, and C because so far the future isn't looking all that great. But is this really dreaming?

Dreams are more like yearnings and desires deeply rooted in one's soul; what I'm doing is more like creating contingency plans.

How can I "dream again" right now? Doesn't God see all the turmoil, the messy, painful, chaos that the world is in? It seems rude and almost sacrilegious to dream of good things when so much bad is happening. I feel it would be better to wait until better days to dream of happiness. So maybe I can keep the idea but shelve it until things are calmer, more stable.

But Moses didn't wait for less dangerous times to dream of freedom for his people. How much agony was his world in when he told the Israelites, "You will be free!"?

Daniel didn't put off the dream of his people entering Jerusalem again, even though he never did. He lived as a captive his whole life, yet his people did return home.

Jesus didn't wait for the chaos that was Israel under Rome to be quelled before He walked out His dream on earth. His dream is still being fulfilled because He died to see it happen.

Dreams aren't just wispy substances that glimmer and hold nothing. Dreams are the things that propel us forward when the present is too hard to understand them. They are worth fighting to keep and even worth pouring our whole lives in them.

True dreams are God-given; they are aspirations that push us to create, to quell chaos, to act not on base instinct but Spirit-driven purpose. Our dreams can become our life's work.

It's time to dream again and I will dare to do it.

I often wonder what You were thinking when you created me. Did you realize that the jet-black hair I had would eventually be dyed into beautiful colors? You thought of every detail, even down to my two slightly webbed feet. You knew that even with those I still wouldn't be able to swim.

It was You who crafted my fiery desire for true justice. How much did You chuckle while crafting my comedic traits? You placed a piece of Your heart in mine; a fierce desire to protect others coupled with the empathy to understand hurts.

How it must have hurt You to see this wonderful work of art slashed and blotched. Your creation hurting itself and throwing ugly shades of noxious colors over the once beautiful canvas. The vibrant hues of justice and protection darkened with hatred; violence splashing over empathy and hiding gentleness.

Once my destructive tantrum passed still You were there; You never left. You started cleaning the destroyed canvas of me bit by bit. Scrubbing off ugly colors, resealing the matting, and stitching little cuts. I didn't look the same though, there were rough spots and blended colors that didn't exist before.

You kept working and telling me how amazing I was but I couldn't quite believe it was true. I listened though, and kept focusing on You until one day I looked down, shocked by what I saw. Through the rough areas and stitched cuts, bleeding over the dark colors, I could see Your beautiful creation shining through. In fact, the flaws only accentuated Your true beauty of art.

You knew exactly what You were doing when You created me. Every stroke, brush, freckle, and character trait were part of Your intricate design. Even the harshness of life couldn't take away the talent You poured out.

I am Your masterpiece, created by You simply because You wanted me.

Twenty-one years ago, Americans went to bed never knowing that the morning would change their world forever.

For millions it would become a day synonymous with an evil and cowardly act.

For thousands it would be their last.

For one man it would be the day his entire life would be summed up in two words: "Let's roll."

Tomorrow marks another September 11th, another year commemorating those lost that awful day.

Tomorrow we will head off to Sunday services, gathering with fellow Christians to worship and pray.

While we remember September 11th, 2001, let's also remember that small group of men and women who fought back.

They chose to take their final moments of life and not go down without a fight.

Church, it's time to get back in the fight.

It's time Church, let's roll!

You are good.
When the days are beautiful.
When children's laughter bubbles out.
You are good.
When grief pours in on every side.
When the sun is dampened with sadness.
Still, I will proclaim, "You are good!"
Through the joy.
Through the loss.
When I can scream it.
Or when I can barely whisper it.
You are good.
When I can see clearly.
And when I can't understand.
I believe and I stand on this truth.
You are a good, good God.

I saw you.

The you who used to be me.

You waved at me from the corner, peeked out from inside the store, and snickered at my discomfort from that old apartment.

The shame of all my past mistakes waving like a knife giving me cuts and slashes.

Your enjoyment at watching who I now am react with horror and disgust at who I once was.

And for a moment I believed you; because after all this is accurate.

You weren't lying; every indignity, each painful action, and the ugliness of such brokenness are all real.

A life of humiliation debased to its core; that was me.

And you enjoyed watching as I remembered every part of it.

But that isn't the whole truth; I didn't stop there in the sewer of self-hatred.

Yeah it hurt, stung something fierce, but that knife isn't as sharp as it used to be.

I tripped and stumbled but something stopped me from falling into the abyss.

Well, not something; Someone.

The same Someone who broke through the prison my mind was trapped in; the One who whispered, "I'll never leave you" and proves His word good every day.

The me I used to be is true but it isn't Truth.

The truth is I'm no longer that person.

Not because I clawed my way out of my shame but because I choose to listen to Truth.

My past me is still me but she lives only in my memory.

I've been set free by God Almighty and even if I occasionally slip
and look back, I won't ever turn back.
I'm never going back and I'm never gonna change my mind.

God could have created humanity to be perfect, so why make us so imperfect?

Why be God of the flawed creations?

Broken, dented, scraped yet imprinted with His very image.

He delights in a creation that can't achieve perfection.

This must mean He delights in the process of our becoming more perfect rather than instantaneously achieving it.

God would rather walk through our messy humanity than snap His fingers and make everything alright.

It's in the mess, the redo's, the brokenness, that we really understand His character.

"I'll never leave you or forsake you."

In the ugliness, the division, the relapses, the bankruptcies, pandemics, even in death.

Never leave you.

God takes our half-painted lives and creates beautiful masterpieces.

Each color swirled in mess matches perfectly in an array of palettes woven together.

Our imperfect designs become His masterpiece.

*I wrote this after a prayer time in my church. We were finally able to come back to the alters without masks and spacing mandated by our city. It was a moment so breathtaking that I could only write a little bit, it was just that overwhelming.

A beautiful wreckage.

Bodies strewn all around.

Some moving, some still.

A few twitch and writhe; while others utter occasional sobs or yells.

What an amazing place, this hallowed ground.

The altar where lives are restored and death is destroyed.

A peaceful carnage, this battlefield where God's Presence tangibly resides.

You call me your King and Father, so what does that make you? As my children, you have the right, no, the responsibility to rule. It is your inheritance and your duty.

As your Father, I delight in watching you grow. As your King, I long for the day when you walk in maturity.

Connect with Me! Learn from Me. I desire with a Father's heart for you to walk in the royalty you are!

You long for My Kingdom on the earth but not more than I do! You're the only part of earth that I created in My own image! Don't shrink from maturity now. Be My Kingdom!

For years I soothed you.

When you were unsettled or angry, I made little concessions, did things your way.

Always made sure you were comfortable over me.

Played music to calm you or rile you; whatever I needed in the moment.

I thought I owned you, that you listened to what I said.

For a while you did; you let me think I was in charge.

That the music my heart played directed you, but in reality you were orchestrating the music.

Like Saul, I thought my demons could be soothed with the right melody.

So I sat content to let you reside over me.

Until one day I realized, I was chained and you no longer cared what music I played.

You didn't care whether I was comfortable, happy, or even sane.

As I sat trying to keep you pacified; you came and draped me in chains.

Now I know the truth, lulling you only puts me to sleep.

I won't live that lie anymore.

My heart's music now belongs to Another; He has destroyed your grip on me.

I won't stand to let you be soothed; instead I've partnered with God to kill you.

My heart's melody is now a war cry coming for you.

I used to wonder how people in captivity sometimes couldn't handle being free. Stockholm Syndrome, identifying with their captors; how did that happen? And then I was captured not by people but by my own mind. Whispers and voices that pulled me down and chained me to the darkest parts of my soul.

The worst part was I didn't even know I was shackled. I walked around for years stumbling over my chains unable to understand the prison I was in.

Suddenly, I was offered freedom. I hadn't asked for it but I took it. I grasped the hand of the One who silences demons and breaks chains.

It was then that I realized why some people stay captured. I was free and now in freedom I had to make decisions. Imprisoned people don't have responsibility; they simply do as they're told. A kind of mindless existence, painful at times but easy. Slipping back into dissociation, listening to the mind voices, and constantly needing others to help me do everything, these were such easy decisions. To be free I had to learn to say yes and no, to accept my decisions had consequences, and learn to trust myself again. It was an impossibility; I couldn't do all these hard things!

Until one day I looked down and realized, I was still holding the chains.

They weren't on my wrists but I hadn't dropped them. I had a choice, keep them or leave them somewhere. So, I left them right

Chains of Freedom

at the place where Freedom entered my life. I took my chains and dropped them in front of the One who silences demons and breaks chains.

Some days those old enemies still whisper to me, but I have encountered Freedom and I will not let Him go.

I am a warrior woman but I am not a feminist.

I am not afraid to be exactly who God made me; from soldier to daughter.

I refuse any labels that call me anything other than what He calls me; redeemed, restored, His beautiful creation.

Like Esther, I intercede for my people with action that saves a nation.

I am a lioness who can also cuddle a crying child.

The same hands that wage war in the heavenlies; give comfort and care to the most vulnerable.

My praise rips the heavens open and provides safety for the wounded to rest.

Like Jael, I can be at home and still use tent stakes to kill evil ones.

I am fierce but not fighting men; we are each uniquely created by God.

Godly men are not toxic, they are exactly who God created them to be, masculine.

I will not demean their masculinity by asserting my femininity over or onto them.

Like Ruth, I'm not looking for "my" Boaz but I'm not afraid if I find him.

I am confident enough to refuse to compete with other women.

We are sisters, not opposing teams, I react with joy when others accomplish life goals.

I will war with and for you, not at you.

Like Elizabeth, the blessing within me leaps with joy when I see yours come to fruition.

I am redeemed and fully free but I don't keep it for myself.

A gift freely offered to me that I now give to others; I will not
    shame anyone for the choices they have made.
I understand desperation and the awful things desperate people
    can do, but I also know a God desperate to walk with you.
Like Rehab, I also have been in the midst of destruction; I am not
    content to save only me, you are part of my family too.

Your eyes look so much like mine. They're still brown but give it time, they'll turn hazel and green. There is so much joy there but sadness lingers too. In less than one month your mom is getting married. The excitement of having a dad is both thrilling and terrifying.

In Cinderella, the step-mother was wicked; is that the same for new daddies too? Or worse, what if he leaves?

What if you and your mom are left alone again? Not to fear, I'm here to tell you that 30 years later he is still here and tells you (and your brothers too) and your mom every night, "I love you." You don't believe this truth yet and I know this because you are me and I am you.

Your smile, while happy, hides the words you keep hearing. "You're too much like a boy! You talk too much! You're not like any other girls." Are they true? How does one be like a girl? Why is talking reprehensible? There you go again talking off on a tangent, using words far too big for such a little girl. I want to warn you, to tell you things not to do as you grow. I want to spare you from any pain. But I can't, because what you don't know is, you are me and I am you.

Our smiles match, our eyes do too (even if the color won't for another year or two). I can't tell you what to look out for or who to befriend (and who not to). It's too late to warn you that words can be more destructive than actions. Yet as I sit here and look at you, there are still some things I want to say to you:

"Tomboys are just extra strong women."

"Talking has saved you from many violent situations."

"You dared to be different and this will eventually make people more comfortable around you."

"You are beautiful."

"I love you."

Even as the tears fall, I know these statements to be true; for you are me and I am you.

It happened again today, halfway thru a workout.

For a moment today you weren't just a boxing bag.

You were a thousand faces all with the same look of hatred.

You were the addiction I chose over my career.

You were labels along with a bag of pills.

You were an old relationship that began and ended in an overdose.

You were me.

Until I remembered that I'm not that person anymore.

That me no longer exists and I can stay stuck punching ghosts on
a boxing bag or move on, finish my boxing class and get on
with my day.

I choose that.

I choose to let my past highlight what God can do with a
surrendered life; not pretend they were my "glory days."

I choose to live as a new creation.

*2021 took many dear friends from our church almost all in the space of two months' time. It was a tough time and not just for my grieving friends, the world seemed to be in mourning. This poured out of me one afternoon. Grief is necessary but it's really for us; our friends now see Jesus face-to-face.

I won't say don't cry for me because crying is a part of healing.
Just remember I haven't completely left.
I'm in your memories, heart, dreams, and laughter.
I've simply gone on ahead, started the next chapter of Kingdom living before you.
Like moving from one place to another; I'm gone but not erased.
When you mourn, because at times you will, try not to let it engulf you.
I have become part of the Heavenly host and am surrounded by all those who came before.
I cry, "Honor, glory and power to God most High" and see Him face to face daily.
We won't always be apart.
One day you too will go ahead of others or the Kingdom will fully encompass the earth.
We will see each other again.
I have simply gotten home before you.

The War Writings

It took decades for me to begin to come to the depths of my deployments. Writing became the outlet for my ripped soul to mend. These are writings that God used to show me that I might have something of substance to give to others. Thankfully, He didn't stop at just these.

1.26

It's not the APR on the new car you want.

It's not a percentage rate for a new credit card, mattress, or mortgage.

It's the military cop who never got to be a wife

It's the infantryman who will never hear the words "Grandpa come play."

It's the brother who never became an uncle.

It's the cousin who never finished college.

It's friends in foxholes who were handed "just in case" letters.

It's rapid fire promises followed by "don't you dare die on me" commands.

It's most definitely not the best bargain you can find on tv, online, or in person.

It's 1.26 million life stories who were cut short, ended before they ever really started.

It's families forever changed.

True Freedom

I fought for freedom once and I lost. I left with grand ideas and intentions of spreading freedom. I returned with a jaded outlook, bitter spirits, and distrust of all people.

I gave no freedom, only rules and punishment.

I fought for freedom once and I lost. Two deployments in two countries, I was sent to free and empower. Instead I watched as men were herded into overflowing prison camps, and I treated them like trash.

I allowed no freedom, only harsh words and cruel indifference.

I fought for freedom once and I lost. I traveled the world and never saw freedom won. When I came home I never truly returned; part of me was still back there fighting ghosts.

I no longer allowed freedom for myself, convinced I no longer had a heart.

I fought for freedom once and I lost. Everywhere I looked freedom was just a shadow, ever moving and fading. And then I heard of a freedom that comes from surrender. I remembered the God from my youth; He promised a freedom from sin but I must give up my authority as exchange.

I was allowed no freedom anyhow, so what could I lose?

I fought for freedom once and I lost. I lost the years of running, defying, and dishonoring God; in one instant I called out and He saved me. Anger, voices, and death fled as He swooped in and began to change my heart of rock into the soft, malleable one it was always supposed to be. So yes, I fought for freedom once and lost, and from that loss I gained victory.

For Michael Pursel 4/14/88-5/6/07

I cried for you today. It only took 12 years. We officially don't have a war in Iraq anymore, but because of you and thousands of others, we never forget what a price war costs.

I cried for you today. 12 years was actually longer than the entire war but trust me none of the tears went bad. They were saved up in a place where no one could reach. I put them in such a sacred place even I wasn't allowed to shed them.

I cried for you today. 12 years after hearing about what happened, stuck in a place where I couldn't grieve. 11 years after almost dying while drinking to your memory; I realize now that you never would want to be remembered that way.

I cried for you today. 12 years later and each drop brought a fond memory and healing. While I hid them out of my reach; God kept them safe for the day that I could let them out and not remember the pain of your passing but just the beauty of your life.

We were boys and girls whose grandpas told them stories of Vietnam, jungle traps, and Agent Orange.

We were sons and daughters whose moms and dads spoke of Operation Desert Storm, oil fires, and a religion most didn't understand.

We grew up in the land of the free and the home of the brave, unafraid. The word terror was a foreign concept.

But you were the brave, the reason we still live in the land of the free.

We were as one after that brutal September morning; marching off war, for justice.

But you were the brave, destined to fight and horrifically to fall.

We were as one and so often in my mind we still are, but the war is done and you are gone.

But you were the brave, you forever will be.

You get told that war will change you; that your mind might get screwed up.

But no one ever tells you that there are moments in war that take you back to fond childhood memories. That the acrid smoke from guns and grenades will momentarily drop you off in recollections of smoke grenades and bottle rockets.

No one ever tells you that war can have hilarious moments which combined with adrenaline turn laughter into a mocking bark of insanity. Like a mad dash across an open field to escape a porta-potty during a rocket attack. Or the difficulty in explaining how almost getting caught on fire three times is actually quite funny.

War takes the normal things in life and twists them into a perverse new interpretation. It often does so in the most violent fashion so that one simply forgets the normalcy of life before war.

It twists celebrations of freedom into reminders of your worst days.

It rewires humor to enjoy a little pain in laughter.

But it also takes ordinary people and creates heroes.

It shows that character may bend but humor is still in the darkest places.

Both the good and bad memories can exist; one doesn't have to swallow the other.

That even though war will change you; it doesn't have to kill you when you come home.

We can struggle with fireworks and still enjoy them.

We don't know each other; you may not even remember me. Well somehow, I doubt that.

Neither one of us was having a good day; how could we, a prisoner and hot-headed guard?

I don't know why you were there and frankly, after all this time, I don't even care.

I was just mad that you wouldn't look at me or answer my questions.

You probably couldn't even understand them.

People always wonder why I dislike May so much.

It's not the riots and prison violence, although there was plenty of that.

It isn't the fact that I lost two friends in a week but that does rank pretty high.

It's you.

Your face and eyes that I see over and over.

Every. Single. May Day.

Mourning on Memorial Day is hard.

But it's easy in comparison to seeing you.

I can still see my face reflected in your eyes.

The hatred, the animalistic glee of hurting you.

I actually felt joyful about your pain.

My life is very different now and I'm sure yours is too.

Like Paul, I had a sudden meeting with God. Everything has changed and yet I still see you.

I often wonder what shock and horror Paul must have felt when he realized the depths of his actions against Stephen and others.

Even with a new life in God, I'm betting he still saw their faces from time to time.

But Paul stated that "nothing can keep us from the love of God," so I'm grabbing hold of that faith too.

We may never meet again you and I, but I have one desperate thing to say to you:

I'm sorry.

It's all I have to give but it's everything to me.
And now I'm going to let you go, your face and eyes.
Even if I still see them occasionally.

I have finally forgiven me.

May seems just too pretty a month to die.

Back home the dogwoods are in bloom, the trees are green again.

The weather is alive with sun, rain, tornadoes, and excitement.

New life is springing up everywhere.

But not here. Here the smell of filth lies as deep as the trash on the roadside.

The only green is in tattered palm tree leaves blown apart by debris flung from roadside bombs.

The flash and bang of another IED springs up, devouring a convoy.

Instead of new life, here in May, men and women die.

19 doesn't seem grown enough to die.

Back home, 19-year-olds gradually age from children to men.

They have years to learn manhood, character, and develop families.

They love May, with its graduations and the promise of new life.

But not here. Here, teens become adults in a boom; explosions forge your character.

You get seconds to prepare for life and death; you age by minutes not years.

Here the month of May becomes synonymous with death not life.

And here, boys of 19 remain forever young; carried home in flag-draped caskets.

The war is over now and time marches on.
We are home and living peaceful lives; most of the time.

Except in May where we once again transport decades back to relive moments when life was uncertain and friendships hadn't yet tasted death.

We grow older but you remain forever 19.

I just realized that I don't wish I could take your place.

Don't get me wrong, I don't like the fact that you died.

But somewhere in the last 15 years I dropped the guilt of being alive.

I still remember you; I can't and don't ever want to forget you.

But I'm going to live; I'm going to enjoy my life made richer because of your sacrifice.

No, I don't hold on to the idealism of dying for one's country as the high point of patriotism.

You didn't want to die for America, you wanted to live for her; yet you willingly paid the cost when it was asked.

Because of you, I know the incredibly high and crushing price that is on a family.

But I'm going to live; I'm going to stop being guilty for surviving when neither one of us had a choice in the matter.

Instead of remembering the anguish of today and the soldier who violently died; I'm going to remember the boy who I grew up with, who had piercing blue eyes and an indomitable spirit.

The boy who went from playing soldier to the man who volunteered to deploy at 18.

I don't want to take your place, Mike, but my friends and family will know who you were.

Because I'm going to live and tell your story.

I thought I might actually make it through May and June without my brain and body colliding in weird flashes. It's hard to explain a mind that believes and knows God has restored it and a body that still reacts to old memories. It's quite literally the past and the present warring in one vessel. But I thought this might be the year that it didn't happen; that I could "prove" to myself that I was truly healed.

Except as many people have noticed, my speech has been more garbled than usual. Telltale sign of stress and anxiety for me. I love words and while I occasionally mix them up, May is a time period where this occurrence goes off the charts.

Until a series of balloon explosions sent me to the point where I could taste sand and feel a red-hot sun. For a moment the past blended with the present, just a second and no more but, for my body it was a second too long.

Or the other day when a nap ended with a huge explosion that brought me screaming back to reality. I thought the bottom of our house had been ripped open. One panicky text to my mother brought the realization that not only was the house perfectly safe but no such noise had even occurred. A dream gone wrong apparently; but I could feel the shaking and pressure from the blast wave in my chest.

"But some of you were once like that. But you were cleansed; you were made holy; you were made right with God by calling on the name of the Lord Jesus Christ and by the Spirit of our God" 1 Corinthians 6:11.

Scripture doesn't say when I feel like it, when my body no longer remembers trauma, or as soon as my brain unscrambles itself, then I'm fully saved. It's when I committed myself to Him, that instant forever frozen in time as the moment of my healing. My brain and body will catch up but I am redeemed whether I fully feel or understand it.

My spirit was made alive in that moment; the rest is just window-dressing.

So bring it on May and June, my God is more than able to handle you.

These men and women didn't head off to war expecting to die. They left knowing that death was a possibility but mostly for "some other guy." This is what makes them heroes. Not a glamorous Hollywood-type death, those things don't exist. Yet the threat of death didn't stop them from still doing their mission.

It's easy for those of us who did come home to get swallowed in Memorial Day. To us and so many families it isn't a "nice" holiday, but it's faces of friends, spouses, parents, and children who are gone forever. We are the mark they left in the world and that can be a heavy, heavy burden.

Saying thanks just isn't enough when remembering the childhood friend who was barely 19, or the man who volunteered for a 4th deployment while still on his 3rd one. But what can I do, give, or say to honor them? Sitting alone, depressed on a holiday meant to commemorate them seems misguided and disgraceful.

I can honor them by living a full life, like the one they wanted to have. No, I can't live for them but in living I can make sure they are never forgotten. I can say thanks to Mike, John, Adam, and the countless men and women. My thank you comes in reconnecting with my family, addressing PTSD, and most importantly establishing a true relationship with God. Because of your sacrifice, my life has gone on.

15 years later I can still feel the heat. Iraq in June is always in the 100's but this day it easily hit above 135. Not a breath of wind. Not even when the rockets landed on base and in the compounds did a whiff of air stir. I didn't worry that I might die from the explosions because I was certain I was slowly baking from the inside out.

June 9, 2007 redefined what my body and brain understood about heat and death.

No air moved not even in an outdoor prison filled with 20,000+ people. As the gates clanged behind us, it felt like walking into an open grave. How could that many people be so utterly silent? In that moment, I was more afraid than all the riots I had been in; even the ones where I was almost lit on fire. The sulfurous, cordite smell hung thick in the middle compounds; sitting like a haze over a row of dead bodies.

June 9 fused the smells of explosions and fear in my brain forever.

But we were alive, no Americans were injured. Well, that's what official reports say; my good friend's brain injury and concussion says otherwise. Airmen sitting around in shocked silence, faces frozen in a daze spoke volumes. The injuries were just beginning. A shrapnel wound, a lost limb are terrible but how does one heal a scrambled brain or a shattered soul? I quickly understood that these people were casualties even though it would take some a long time before they realized it. It took me over a decade to realize I was one too.

June 9 forever changed the way I understood trauma but it doesn't define me or my friends.

Faces flash before me- young, vibrant, and tragically gone.

Friends snatched too soon.

Accidents, war, sickness, murder…suicide.

The last one hurts extra because it was preventable.

Why them? Why not me, I'm not extra special.

After all I've been there and had that dance with the Reaper.

Each time I hear of another one gone, that thought stabs again.

It's a question I let settle with a simple I'll never know.

And it goes away, until the next face pops up.

I may never know but I do know one thing: As long as I have breath, I'll remember you.

Your names will still be spoken and not just on holidays.

I'll remember the funny and stupid things along with the heroic and tragic.

We are forever brothers and sisters, alive and fallen- bonded through flight lines and battlegrounds, deployments and TDYs and one oath.

We'll remember you all; accidents, war, sickness, murder, even suicide will never dampen your memories, you will live on.

What so many people don't understand is while they moved on, we were stuck everyday remembering two towers falling. Our military core smoking and in ruins. A gash of land in Pennsylvania. The last words of Todd Beamer actually became some unit's motto: "Let's Roll."

We left our homeland to right those wrongs and in return it felt like she left us over there and moved onto other things.

While many of us were off in very foreign lands, our homeland became foreign to us. We returned home to our childhood heroes being shot, mocked, and told they were useless. If my country could treat our homeland's first responders this way, how would they treat us, the nation's first responders?

Veteran homelessness blossomed overnight, many of us would rather be on the streets than face people we simply couldn't understand. Alcohol and drug use grew followed by jail sentences.

We had our answer, the public now thought we, yesterday's heroes, were today's monsters.

So we insulated. We told no civilians our stories, kept them safe to ourselves even as they ate away at our souls. Suicide rates doubled then tripled.

There were many times when I wished I had died over there rather than come home.

The only "safe" people were our buddies, and they were struggling too; death notifications came monthly, sometimes weekly.

Everyone else was suspect, especially our own families. The VA hospitals swelled and spilled broken people everywhere because they simply couldn't treat everyone.

But now our foreign wars are done, at least physically.

It's time to stop waging the war against our families and civilian populace. Many of them truly want to help, they just don't know how. My veteran brothers and sisters, it's time to bridge the gap; it's literally killing us when we don't. We've set up the idea of being a monster for so long, we don't know how to be a person. Our friends and family do. Let them in, not everyone is suspect.

We marched into hell together, now let's walk out together.

The war is over, it's time to come home.

I lost more than I can fully ever know in that desert sand. Naivete was demolished but I never realized how much innocence was taken as well. The more I try and pinpoint where it happened the more it slips through my brain like sand on a dusty day.

It could have been in the first riot or the last; the screams and chants of angry men bruised more than the rocks and pellets smacking my body armor.

Maybe it was the shadowy mirage of power; the intoxicating thrill to give pain or make it stop. Like a drug, it wouldn't stop at one time and the cost was more than I understood.

Perhaps it was seeing the evil people could do to each other all in the name of the same god. Ten months of tasting what the Crusades were like; each side declaring their version of god was better while attempting to beat the other into extinction.

How ironic that the Cradle of Civilization is where a large part of me died while the rest became a wild monster.

But it didn't stay that way.

It took eleven more years of wandering in the desert of my mind before I finally came home. Eleven years of living mentally and sometimes physically like an animal; caged but thinking I was free.

Finally, I met Truth, not the petty god being fought over, but the real One who came to give freedom and restore monsters back to humanity.

The God Nebuchadnezzar met in the wilderness of Babylon.

The Truth who ended the Israelites 40 years of wandering.

The Savior that turned a murderous Pharisee into a humble man named Paul.

I may never fully know all that I lost in that desolate sandbox and that's ok. It drove me to the point of death, which is where I found Life waiting for me.

The desert winds still blow across my mind but now I'm no longer lost in the storm. When I stumble, I trip into nail-pierced hands that hold me until the storm swirls past.

The desert can keep the old animal me.

I've been brought back to life by Life Himself, and I'm done staying purposefully in the sandstorms of my past.

What is a moral injury?

It's the outrage of seeing a single man being beaten by a mob and there is nothing you can do to stop it. Day after day it continues until you're finally so numb you take bets on how long each beating lasts.

It's the horror of hearing men "welcomed" to prison. Or maybe it's getting so accustomed to it that you laugh about it.

It's no longer being worried about violent riots and hard pushes but enjoying them because you no longer have to exercise restraint-you can finally vent all the stress you've built up. The adrenaline rush of causing someone pain becomes an intoxicating drug.

It's seeing a monster holding a gun reflected in someone's eyes and realizing the monster is you.

It's coming back to the land of normal people, loving and hating them because they seem naïve and happy. Knowing it's good that they are happy and hating them because you can't be anymore.

It's hearing/seeing every terrible thing you couldn't stop every time someone calls you a hero. What hero just allows injustice day after day?

Pretty words and nice scientific phrases cannot accurately describe it. A moral injury is a ripping of the heart, a shredding of the soul, and a broken spirit. It whispers the only way to silence the agony is to be silenced. This injury points the wounded in only one direction: death.

Thankfully, I know a Physician who takes delight in healing not only body wounds but mental, spiritual, and soul ones as well.

So when a child's happy scream conjures up images of brutality I don't have to stay in that terrifying memory. My Father is the Healer.

When a well-meant word about my service makes me cringe remembering every dishonorable thing; I remind myself my God is my Redeemer.

Against all psychological reasoning, my wound is healing. The injuries inflicted by the atrocities of being unable to help others in need and letting myself fall into evil are being eradicated. The poison is being sucked out.

This moral injury is one that will not control my life any longer.

What's it like being a veteran?

Being a veteran is weird. I grew up in a military town and I don't remember any big hoopla over November 11th. Sure, there was maybe a town parade but definitely no free dinners or stuff unless you went to the VFW's free lunch.

Veteran. I hear the word and automatically look around for an older guy that fits my mental description of that word. Not me; I'm too young. Most days I still feel like a wild and carefree 20-year-old. At least in my head I do; my back and knees remind me I'm not.

It's even weirder when I realize I never knew what a peacetime military looked like. The Air Force I joined was already in one war and entered another pretty quickly. I didn't join to go to college or see the world; I wanted to kill the people who had hurt my country. It's an odd thing for which to be thanked; having a bloodthirsty desire for revenge. Any other job where you have that mindset will either get you locked up in prison or a psych ward, definitely not thanked.

There are entire portions of years that I don't remember, heck I've even forgotten my birthday, holidays, etc. Ask me about Christmas in Okinawa or the 4th of July in Iraq, zero recall of anything about those days.

But there are other days that I can remember with crystal clarity. A long, flooded march in basic training, putting on MOPP gear on a hot flight line in Okinawa, frostbite in North Dakota, and breathtaking sunrises in Pakistan.

Every May 6 and 14, I remember two men who will never age another day.

On June 9 don't be surprised to find me extra jumpy, explosions and mayhem are seared into my psyche.

But now my wars are over; good or bad, they are done. That doesn't mean we aren't still dying from them.

I know more friends who have died by suicide than in combat.

Just because a war is declared finished doesn't mean it's completed; it can live on for years and sometimes forever in hearts and minds. The bad memories and the good are tied hand-in-hand so I keep them both because I can't comprehend the thought of not having either.

So yeah, being a veteran is amazing, beautiful, painfully complex, and especially weird.

Made in the USA
Coppell, TX
11 February 2023

12635549R00088